Complete and Incomplete Econometric Models

Complete and Incomplete Econometric Models

John Geweke

Princeton University Press
Princeton and Oxford

Published by Princeton University Press,
41 William Street, Princeton, New Jersey 08540

In the United Kingdom: Princeton University Press,
6 Oxford Street, Woodstock, Oxfordshire OX20 1TW

Library of Congress Cataloging-in-Publication Data

Geweke, John.
Complete and incomplete econometric models / John Geweke.
p. cm. — (The Econometric and Tinbergen Institutes lecture series)
Includes bibliographical references.
ISBN 978-0-691-14002-5 (hardcover : alk. paper)
1. Econometric models. I. Title.
HB141.G49 2010
330.01'5195—dc22 2009024293

British Library Cataloging-in-Publication Data is available

This book has been composed in LucidaBright using TEX
Typeset and copyedited by T&T Productions Ltd, London

Printed on acid-free paper. ∞

press.princeton.edu

Printed in the United States of America

10 9 8 7 6 5 4 3 2 1

Contents

Series Editors' Introduction

The Econometric and Tinbergen Institutes Lectures deal with topics in econometrics that have important policy implications. The lectures cover a wide range of topics and are not confined to any one area or subdiscipline. Leading international scientists in the fields of econometrics in which applications play a major role are invited to give three-day lectures on a topic to which they have contributed significantly.

The topic of model construction is one of the most challenging subjects in the economic sciences. In the present book John Geweke starts from the well-known assumption that all models are false in the sense of not fully describing the economic process under consideration but that some models are useful for a particular decision problem. In an innovative approach Geweke treats a Bayesian analysis of how to deal with incomplete econometric models in a predictive and decision-making context.

As editors of the series we are indebted to the Tinbergen Institute for continued support for the series.

Philip Hans Franses and Herman K. van Dijk
Econometric and Tinbergen Institutes
Erasmus School of Economics

Preface

This book elaborates the substance of the Econometric and Tinbergen Institutes Lectures that I presented at Erasmus University Rotterdam in June 2008. I am grateful to the Econometric Institute, Princeton University Press, and especially to Herman van Dijk for this opportunity to synthesize themes in my research program from the past decade. I am indebted to several anonymous reviewers for their comments, and to Gianni Amisano for collaboration on research related to chapter 5. The National Science Foundation supported this work through grant SBR-0720547.

Chapter 1 describes the context and theme for the volume and should be accessible to a wide audience. Chapter 2 provides background in Bayesian econometrics that should prove useful to readers with graduate education in economics but not specifically in Bayesian econometrics. It also establishes notation that is used throughout the rest of the book. The remaining chapters are three essays that can be read independently of one another. They are presented together here in the belief that the reader who persists through all three will conclude, as I have, that incomplete models are effective research tools. There are, undoubtedly, instances beyond those described here in which incomplete models will provide fresh perspectives on applied econometrics. It would be most gratifying if publication of this book leads to further research in this direction.

1
Introduction

Models are the venue for expressing, comparing, and evaluating alternative ways of addressing important questions in economics. Applied econometricians are called upon to engage in these exercises using data and, often, formal methods whose properties are understood in decision-making contexts. This is true of work in other sciences as well.

There is a large literature on alternative formal approaches to these tasks, including both Bayesian and non-Bayesian methods. Formal approaches tend to take models as given, and the more formal the approach the more likely this is to be true. Whether the topic is inference, estimation, hypothesis testing, or specification testing, the formal treatment begins with a specific model. The same is also true of formal approaches to the tasks of prediction and policy evaluation.

Yet the ultimate success of these endeavors depends strongly on creativity, insight, and skill in the process of model creation. As the model builder entertains new ideas, casting off those that are not deemed promising and developing further those that are, he or she is engaged in a sophisticated process of learning. This process does not, typically, involve the specification of a great many models developed to the point of departure assumed in formal treatments in graduate courses, texts in econometrics and statistics, and journal articles. Discarding models that would ultimately be unsuccessful earlier rather than later in this process of learning improves the allocation of research time and talent.

Model development is inherently a task of learning under conditions of unstructured uncertainty. To assume that one's model fully accounts for the phenomenon under question is naive. A more defensible position is that of Box (1980): all models are wrong, but some are useful. To this it might be added that, with inspiration and perspiration, models can be improved. The process of information acquisition, learning, and behavior when objectives are well-specified in a utility or loss function is familiar ground in economics. In modeling the optimal behavior of economic agents in this situation the dominant paradigm is Bayesian learning, to the point that many in the profession are comfortable terming such behavior rational.

Can this paradigm be applied to model development? A number of obstacles suggest that the task may be demanding. First, the behavior of practicing econometricians regularly appears inconsistent with the Bayesian learning paradigm. In particular, the dominant statistical paradigm in econometrics has been frequentist and the inconsistencies of this approach with Bayesian inference and learning are well-known. Second, Bayesian model specification is more demanding than most non-Bayesian model specification, requiring prior distributions for inherently unobservable constructs like parameters, as well as for models themselves when multiple models are under consideration. Finally, whereas in academic treatments of Bayesian learning reality is fully specified, in applying economics to policy questions it is not even clear that the existence of a data-generating process has any epistemological standing at all.

The thesis of this monograph is that these objections can be met, and its essays are explorations of the prospects for more effective use of the Bayesian paradigm at the point where the investigator has much less information than is presumed in formal econometric approaches, be they Bayesian or non-Bayesian. At this point models are inherently incomplete: that is, they are lacking some aspect of a joint distribution over all parameters, latent variables, and models under consideration. Chapter 2 details more fully the concept of a complete model. It also establishes notation and serves as a primer on Bayesian econometrics.

Model incompleteness can take many forms, and the essays in this monograph take up three examples. Chapter 3 addresses the early steps of model construction—before the investigator has engaged the technical demands of formal inference or estimation and perhaps even before data have been collected. The emphasis in this chapter is on using formal Bayesian methods to compare and evaluate models. Model *comparison* at this stage amounts to prior predictive analysis, which was introduced to statistics by Box (1980) and emphasized in econometrics by Lancaster (2004) and Geweke (2005). These ideas are not new, but their potential for greatly accelerating effective research is not as yet well appreciated in the econometrics community. Model *evaluation* is the assessment of a specified model by absolute standards—a process in which economists regularly engage. The assertion, or conclusion, that a model is bad for a particular purpose is repeatedly heard in the economist's workday. But, as economists regularly point out, statements like this raise the question, bad compared with what? The final section of chapter 3 sets up an incomplete model as the basis of comparison implicit in such statements, and then extends the conventional apparatus of Bayesian model comparison to the complete model being evaluated and the incomplete model that is implicitly held as the standard. This treatment provides a fully Bayesian counterpoint to frequentist tests against an unspecified alternative, also known as pure significance testing.

No model is meant to specify all aspects of reality, even a sharply confined reality chosen for its relevance to a particular academic or policy question. This restriction can be straightforward for formal econometrics: for example, the stipulation that a regression model applies only over a specified range of values of the covariates, or that a structural model with several endogenous variables is intended only to provide the marginal distribution of a subset of these variables. But often the restriction is stronger. Chapter 4 takes up the case of structural models that are intended only to provide certain population moments as functions of the structural parameters of the model, a restriction that is especially common in dynamic stochastic general equilibrium models. The chapter shows that widely applied procedures, including conventional calibration, violate this restriction by taking the higher-order moments of the model literally in reaching conclusions about its structural parameters. It provides a constructive approach to this learning problem by treating explicitly the incompleteness of the structural model and then completing the model in a way that relies only on those aspects of the structural model intended to be taken literally. In the example used throughout the chapter this approach reverses widely held conclusions about the incompatibility of the U.S. equity premium with simple growth models.

Formal Bayesian methods provide a logically consistent and well-understood solution to the problem of using competing models with conflicting implications in a decision-making context. The critical element of this solution is the specification of prior model probabilities that sum to one. In so doing, the solution conditions on the process that actually generated the data being one of the models under consideration. Non-Bayesian methods that lead to rules for model choice also make the latter assumption. A widely observed characteristic of the formal Bayesian approach is that it often assigns posterior probability very close to unity for one of the models. The Bayesian solution then effectively amounts to model choice. This is not a problem for econometric theory, because in general the data-generating process is the one selected asymptotically. On the other hand, there is an evident conflict with reality: in reaching important decisions policymakers routinely wrestle with alternative models, leading to an apparent inconsistency of clear evidence with presumed rationality of the decision makers. The final chapter in this monograph steps back from the key assumption that reality lies somewhere in the space of models being considered. Replacing the assumption that the model space is completely specified with the alternative of a linear combination of predictive densities of future events that renders past events most probable, it shows that if the data-generating process is not among the group of models considered, then one will use several models. The weights given to these models will converge to positive limits asymptotically. The weights assigned in Bayesian model averaging are incorrect, under this alternative specification in which the model space is incomplete.

2
The Bayesian Paradigm

The Bayesian paradigm provides a powerful and practical structure for managing the risk inherent in decision making. This chapter discusses the elements of this structure, which is standard in the subjective Bayesian approach to inference and decision making. A number of recent texts provide more detailed consideration of this approach in econometrics, including Poirier (1995), Koop (2003), Lancaster (2004), Geweke (2005), Rossi et al. (2005), and Greenberg (2007). This chapter also reviews the Bayesian literature on model evaluation: the effort to assess whether the structure under consideration corresponds to reality. Model evaluation is an inherently difficult question from a Bayesian perspective, and the rest of this monograph explores some ways this can be done using incomplete models.

The essential element of the Bayesian paradigm is a complete model, detailed in section 2.1. A complete model provides a coherent joint probability distribution for the evidence relevant to the decision, unknown parameters or latent variables in the model, and additional factors that will determine the consequences of the decision but are unknown at the time the decision is made. With this distribution in hand, and a utility function for preferences over all possible consequences of the decision, the decision maker can, in principle, determine the decision that maximizes expected utility conditional on the observed evidence. A complete model, therefore, amounts to the explicit econometric implementation of the classical von Neumann–Morgenstern normative theory of decision making under uncertainty. Advances in computation, and in particular in simulation methods, since 1990 have made this implementation practical using models much more realistic than those that can be used in purely analytical approaches. Section 2.3 briefly reviews the highlights of these advances.

Especially for an important problem in a complex environment, decision makers have before them alternative models. Since the models are all relevant to the decision, each specifies the distribution of the factors determining the consequences of the decision, conditional on alternative decisions that might be made. If all of the models are Bayesian with proper prior distributions, then they are all complete. By specifying prior (that is, unconditional) probabilities on the alternative models, decision makers can extend the coherent probability distributions of the individual models to all of the models under consideration, as described in section 2.2. Since the distribution over observables and factors determining the consequences of alternative decisions is coherent and complete, the familiar expected utility calculus applies. The mechanics of this process impose greater technical demands than do those of a single model. Section 2.2 reviews the substantial progress on this problem that has been made in the past decade.

The specification of the set of Bayesian models under consideration is typically recursive. It begins with a prior probability for each model. Then, within each model, the prior probability distribution of unobservables (parameters and latent variables) is followed by the distribution of observables conditional on unobservables. Finally, each model provides the distribution of factors relevant to the decision conditional on unobservables and observables. There are minor variations on this theme: in particular, the distribution of latent variables and observables conditional on parameters may be more convenient. Regardless, model specification is almost always a forward recursion from models to unobservables to observables to decision-relevant factors. Simulation from this distribution is straightforward, as outlined in section 2.3, and the convenience of this simulation emerges as an important factor in chapters 3 and 4. For a decision maker, however, the relevant distribution is conditional on the data—the observables that are known when the decision is made. This posterior distribution is neither forward nor recursive, and the corresponding simulation is not straightforward. Since the late 1980s extraordinary progress has been made in solving these simulation problems, and these solutions in turn are essential to the ongoing rapid growth in the practical application of complete models to important decisions. Section 2.3 reviews these methods very briefly. They are used only in chapter 5, which requires no detailed understanding of posterior distribution simulators. The texts mentioned at the start of this chapter all provide treatments of that topic in greater depth.

The strength of the Bayesian paradigm is its specification of a complete and coherent structure answering the question: conditional on the models specified, the available data, and a given utility function, what is the appropriate decision? Alternative utility functions provide no essential complication: the paradigm provides the answer for any utility function for which expected utility is known to exist. It can also easily address the sensitivity of the decision to alternative prior distributions of parameters. These are all critical advantages relative to non-Bayesian methods: some additional attractions of Bayesian methods include accounting for parameter uncertainty, avoiding the need to choose a single model from many, and the ability to discover the extent to which disagreements among decision makers are due to different beliefs or different utility functions. Yet, the answer that emerges can be no better than the models under consideration.

The same caveat applies to non-Bayesian methods. Model evaluation, in the form of hypothesis testing, has been central to non-Bayesian statistics since its inception in the late nineteenth century. Within the Bayesian paradigm it is possible to lose sight of the fact that the precise and relevant answers it provides are contingent on the adequacy of its complete models. There is a lively Bayesian literature on the use of predictive distributions to evaluate these models. Section 2.4 reviews these approaches, as do Lancaster (2004) and Geweke (2005), and they provide foundations for the rest of this monograph. Whether or not purely Bayesian methods can be used to evaluate models has long been an open question in this literature. Chapter 3, building on section 2.4, shows that pure Bayesian model evaluation is both possible and practical using incomplete models.

2.1 Complete Models

Denote a complete model by A, “assumptions.” A complete model has four elements:

(1) A $j_T \times 1$ observable random vector $\boldsymbol{y}_T$, where T denotes the sample size. The notation j_T allows flexibility in the specification of $\boldsymbol{y}$. For example, if an $m \times 1$ vector is observable at each of T sample points, then one can write $\boldsymbol{y}_T' = (\tilde{\boldsymbol{y}}_1', \dots, \tilde{\boldsymbol{y}}_T')$ with $j_T = Tm$. Some data may be missing, in which case $j_T \leqslant Tm$ and j_T may be random.

(2) A $k_{A,T} \times 1$ unobservable random vector $\boldsymbol{\theta}_{A,T} \in \Theta_{A,T}$. The vector may consist of parameters, latent variables, or both. The notation $\boldsymbol{\theta}_{A,T}$ reflects the fact that this vector is specific to the model. The dimension $k_{A,T}$ may also depend on T, as is typically the case with latent variables. The number of parameters may also depend on sample size, as is the case with flexible highly parameterized models and with explicitly nonparametric Bayesian models. Missing data can be included in $\boldsymbol{\theta}_{A,T}$.

(3) A $q \times 1$ random vector of interest $\boldsymbol{\omega}_T \in \Omega_T$. This vector includes all of the random variables that enter into the decision maker's utility function, described below. For those decisions that require prediction, $\boldsymbol{\omega}_T$ includes future values of random variables, some or all of which may be observed at a future point in time.

(4) A $p \times 1$ decision vector $\boldsymbol{d}_T \in \mathcal{D}$, consisting of all of the elements of the decision at hand. The vector $\boldsymbol{d}_T$ might include exogenous variables controlled by the decision maker. These might not affect the distribution of $\boldsymbol{\omega}_T$: for example elements of the strategy of a small trader. At the other extreme, elements of $\boldsymbol{d}_T$ could be exogenous variables very important in the distribution of future values of random variables: for example the decisions made by a central bank. The vector $\boldsymbol{d}_T$ can index a policy function in a model that is structural in the sense of Hurwicz (1962).

A complete model has four components, consisting of probability density functions. All are expressed with respect to a measure reflecting the discrete and/or continuous nature of the random vector distributions in question, but that fact is not recognized formally in the notation. Whenever the question arises it will be assumed, only to simplify the notation, that the random vector is continuously distributed.

(1) A probability density of observables conditional on unobservables:

$$p(\boldsymbol{y}_T \mid \boldsymbol{\theta}_{A,T}, A). \tag{2.1}$$

If the vector $\boldsymbol{\theta}_{A,T}$ consists only of parameters, and its length does not depend on sample size so that $\boldsymbol{\theta}_{A,T} = \boldsymbol{\theta}_A$, then $L(\boldsymbol{\theta}_A; \boldsymbol{y}_T^o) = p(\boldsymbol{y}_T^o \mid \boldsymbol{\theta}_{A,T}, A)$ is the likelihood function. The vector $\boldsymbol{y}_T^o$ denotes the realized ex post observable, i.e., data, whereas the vector $\boldsymbol{y}_T$ denotes the random ex ante observable. With more complex structures there may be some discretion in the definition of the likelihood function. For example, the vector of unobservables $\boldsymbol{\theta}_{A,T}$ may consist of parameters $\boldsymbol{\theta}_A$ and latent variables $\boldsymbol{\lambda}_{A,T}$. Then the likelihood function is typically taken to be

$$L(\boldsymbol{\theta}_A; \boldsymbol{y}_T^o) = \int_{\Lambda_{A,T}} p(\boldsymbol{y}_T^o \mid \boldsymbol{\theta}_A, \boldsymbol{\lambda}_{A,T}) p(\boldsymbol{\lambda}_{A,T} \mid \boldsymbol{\theta}_A, A)\, d\boldsymbol{\lambda}_{A,T}.$$

(2) A prior probability density function

$$p(\boldsymbol{\theta}_{A,T} \mid A), \tag{2.2}$$

which expresses reasonable values of the unobservables. This notation includes a rich hierarchy for parameters and latent variables, for example

$$\boldsymbol{\theta}'_{A,T} = (\boldsymbol{\lambda}'_{A,T}, \boldsymbol{\psi}'_A, \boldsymbol{\phi}'_A),$$

with

$$p(\boldsymbol{\theta}_{A,T} \mid A) = p(\boldsymbol{\lambda}_{A,T} \mid \boldsymbol{\psi}_A)p(\boldsymbol{\psi}_A \mid \boldsymbol{\phi}_A)p(\boldsymbol{\phi}_A \mid A);$$

$\boldsymbol{\psi}_A$ is the vector of parameters as usually understood, $\boldsymbol{\phi}_A$ is a vector of hyperparameters in a hierarchical prior distribution with two levels, and $\boldsymbol{\lambda}_{A,T}$ is a vector of latent variables. An essentially unlimited class of variants on this structure is possible, including hierarchical priors with multiple levels. In all cases, the prior distribution expresses the reasonable range of behavior of unobservables that the model is intended to describe.

(3) A probability density of the vector of interest:

$$p(\boldsymbol{\omega}_T \mid \boldsymbol{y}_T, \boldsymbol{\theta}_{A,T}, \boldsymbol{d}_T, A). \tag{2.3}$$

In some cases, the vector $\boldsymbol{\omega}_T$ might consist of certain elements of $\boldsymbol{\theta}_{A,T}$. For example, in a marketing problem the decision might be how to approach potential customers already in the sample and $\boldsymbol{\omega}_T$ would then consist of customer-specific latent variables. If, in the same situation, the decision involved customers drawn randomly from the population but not in the sample, then $\boldsymbol{\omega}_T$ would include latent variables for those customers. In a decision in which prediction of the future is required, $\boldsymbol{\omega}_T$ might include vectors of the form $\boldsymbol{\omega}_T' = (\tilde{\boldsymbol{y}}_{T+1}', \dots, \tilde{\boldsymbol{y}}_{T+f}')$, and if the composition of $\boldsymbol{\theta}_{A,T}$ does not depend on T, then

$$p(\boldsymbol{\omega}_T \mid \boldsymbol{y}_T, \boldsymbol{\theta}_{A,T}, \boldsymbol{d}_T, A)$$
$$= \prod_{s=1}^{f} p(\tilde{\boldsymbol{y}}_{T+s} \mid \tilde{\boldsymbol{y}}_{T+s-1}, \dots, \tilde{\boldsymbol{y}}_{T+1}, \tilde{\boldsymbol{y}}_T^o, \dots, \tilde{\boldsymbol{y}}_1^o, \boldsymbol{\theta}_{A,T}, A). \tag{2.4}$$

The density $p(\boldsymbol{\omega}_T \mid \boldsymbol{y}_T, \boldsymbol{\theta}_{A,T}, \boldsymbol{d}_T)$ can incorporate optimization by forward-looking economic agents who know or are learning a policy indexed by $\boldsymbol{d}_T$.

(4) A utility function $U(\boldsymbol{\omega}_T, \boldsymbol{d}_T)$ that determines the decision

$$\hat{\boldsymbol{d}}_T = \underset{\boldsymbol{d}_T \in \mathcal{D}}{\operatorname{argmax}} \operatorname{E}[U(\boldsymbol{\omega}_T, \boldsymbol{d}_T) \mid \boldsymbol{y}_T^o, A]. \tag{2.5}$$

This notation embraces all decision problems within the classical von Neumann–Morgenstern paradigm. These range from myopic or one-step problems to the discounted time-separable utility functions of infinitely lived agents in conventional dynamic structural models. There is no loss of generality in taking the dimension of $\boldsymbol{\omega}_T$ to be finite, since implemented solutions for such problems generally take this form.

This description of a complete model takes as given the specification of the model A and the availability of evidence in the form of data $\boldsymbol{y}_T^o$. This assumption is standard in formal econometrics but in fact substantial time, skill, and energy are generally required to design A and acquire $\boldsymbol{y}_T^o$ so as to lead to a reliable decision $\hat{\boldsymbol{d}}_T$ given the constraints of actual decision making. The remaining chapters of this monograph are devoted to the specification of A. With A and $\boldsymbol{y}_T^o$ in hand, Bayesian inference consists of three steps.

(1) Using the first two components of the complete model, obtain the posterior density of the unobservables

$$p(\boldsymbol{\theta}_{A,T} \mid \boldsymbol{y}_T^o, A) = p(\boldsymbol{\theta}_{A,T} \mid A) p(\boldsymbol{y}_T^o \mid \boldsymbol{\theta}_{A,T}, A) / p(\boldsymbol{y}_T^o \mid A). \tag{2.6}$$

(2) Introducing the third component of the complete model, obtain the posterior density of the vector of interest

$$p(\boldsymbol{\omega}_T \mid \boldsymbol{y}_T^o, \boldsymbol{d}_T, A) = \int_{\Theta_{A,T}} p(\boldsymbol{\omega}_T \mid \boldsymbol{y}_T^o, \boldsymbol{\theta}_{A,T}, \boldsymbol{d}_T, A)\, p(\boldsymbol{\theta}_{A,T} \mid \boldsymbol{y}_T^o, A)\, \mathrm{d}\boldsymbol{\theta}_{A,T}. \tag{2.7}$$

(3) Bringing in the fourth component of the model, evaluate

$$\mathrm{E}[U(\boldsymbol{\omega}_T, \boldsymbol{d}_T) \mid \boldsymbol{y}_T^o, A] = \int_{\Omega_T} U(\boldsymbol{\omega}_T, \boldsymbol{d}_T)\, p(\boldsymbol{\omega}_T \mid \boldsymbol{y}_T^o, \boldsymbol{d}_T, A)\, \mathrm{d}\boldsymbol{\omega}_T \tag{2.8}$$

for relevant values of $\boldsymbol{d}_T$ and determine $\hat{\boldsymbol{d}}_T$ in (2.5).[1]

All three steps are necessary for formal decision making, but the results of the intermediate steps are often useful and of value in themselves. From (2.6) it is possible to proceed to alternative decision-making problems using different vectors of interest and utility functions, as long as (2.6) is expressed in a way that is accessible. (Section 2.3 addresses accessibility.) For an econometrician engaged in reporting to potential decision makers, (2.6) may be the goal, and many treatments of Bayesian econometrics reflect this perspective. If econometric modeling is to have value within the classical economic framework of decision making under uncertainty, it must be capable of supporting the second and third steps. This objective is important in the approach taken to expressing (2.6) and, even more important, to the specification of A, which is taken up in succeeding chapters.

---

[1] This presumes the existence of (2.8). Section 2.3 returns to this point.

The expression of (2.7) is specific to a decision problem if the distribution of $\boldsymbol{\omega}_T$ actually depends on $\boldsymbol{d}_T$, but in many interesting cases the decision will not affect this distribution. In the marketing example above, in which potential customers are drawn either from the sample or from the population, this is the case. Financial management or trading strategies, in which the decision maker has a negligible effect on future asset prices whose realization determines U, constitute another broad class of examples. In a general sense, if

$$p(\boldsymbol{\omega}_T \mid \boldsymbol{y}_T, \boldsymbol{\theta}_{A,T}, \boldsymbol{d}_T) = p(\boldsymbol{\omega}_T \mid \boldsymbol{y}_T, \boldsymbol{\theta}_{A,T}),$$

then (2.7) is a pure prediction problem. For all such problems, making (2.7) accessible is a valuable step. This is consistent with the robust academic and commercial markets for this activity. If decision making is not a pure prediction problem, then conditional predictions, which amount to finding (2.7) for some alternative interesting values of $\boldsymbol{d}_T$, provide some information bearing on (2.8). If $\mathcal{D}$ consists of just a few points, this comes close to determining $\hat{\boldsymbol{d}}_T$.

2.2 Model Comparison and Averaging

When an important decision is made in an uncertain environment, there may be several models $A_1, \dots, A_n$ available for determining $\hat{\boldsymbol{d}}_T$, each model being entertained seriously in the decision-making process. If the models are complete, the calculus of the previous section can be applied, each model A_j leading to decision $\hat{\boldsymbol{d}}_{T,j}$ for $j = 1, \dots, n$. Suppose that for some pairs of models A_i and A_j it is the case that

$$\mathrm{E}[U(\boldsymbol{\omega}_T, \hat{\boldsymbol{d}}_{T,i}) \mid \boldsymbol{y}_T^o, A_j] \ll \mathrm{E}[U(\boldsymbol{\omega}_T, \hat{\boldsymbol{d}}_{T,j}) \mid \boldsymbol{y}_T^o, A_j], \tag{2.9}$$

where "$\ll$" indicates that, from the perspective of A_j, it would be preferable to maintain the decision vector $\hat{\boldsymbol{d}}_{T,j}$ and give up substantial resources with certainty than to adopt $\hat{\boldsymbol{d}}_{T,i}$ with no further sacrifice of resources. Here "substantial" means large relative to the resources required to develop and implement model A_j; (2.9) is one rendering of importance combined with uncertainty in this environment. In this context, it is the rationale for the expenditure of real resources on modeling and model improvement in central banking, meteorology, epidemiology, and a host of other decision-making contexts.

The uncertain environment arises because of differences in (2.1), (2.2), and/or (2.3) across models, combined with the fact that there is no basis for comparison. The differences in distributions are inherent in the models. The problem in comparison is that there are n separate probability spaces. This difficulty can be addressed readily, at least from a formal perspective, as follows. Denote the supermodel by $A = \{A_1, \dots, A_n\}$, and make the supermodel complete by specifying a prior probability distribution $P(A = A_j \mid A) = p(A_j \mid A)$; this implies $\sum_{j=1}^{n} p(A_j \mid A) = 1$, and without loss of generality $p(A_j \mid A) > 0$ $(j = 1, \dots, n)$.

Since each model is complete, there exist coherent probability densities $p(\boldsymbol{y}_T, \boldsymbol{\theta}_{A_j,T}, \boldsymbol{\omega}_T \mid A_j)$ $(j = 1, \dots, n)$. Consequently,

$$
\begin{aligned}
p(\boldsymbol{y}_T, \boldsymbol{\theta}_{A_1,T}, \dots, \boldsymbol{\theta}_{A_n,T}, \boldsymbol{\omega}_T \mid \boldsymbol{d}_T, A) \\
= \sum_{j=1}^{n} p(A_j \mid A) p(\boldsymbol{\theta}_{A_j,T} \mid A_j) p(\boldsymbol{y}_T \mid \boldsymbol{\theta}_{A_j,T}, A_j) \\
\times p(\boldsymbol{\omega}_T \mid \boldsymbol{y}_T, \boldsymbol{\theta}_{A_j,T}, \boldsymbol{d}_T).
\end{aligned}
\tag{2.10}
$$

The joint distribution in (2.10) leads to the conditional distribution $p(\boldsymbol{\omega} \mid \boldsymbol{y}_T^o, A)$ required for determination of $\hat{\boldsymbol{d}}_T = \operatorname{argmax}_{\boldsymbol{d}_T} \mathrm{E}[U(\boldsymbol{\omega}_T, \boldsymbol{d}_T) \mid \boldsymbol{y}_T^o, A]$.

The steps leading to $\hat{\boldsymbol{d}}_T$ are fairly straightforward and highlight the role of the evidence $\boldsymbol{y}_T^o$ in addressing uncertainty about models. This can be seen directly by working backward. From (2.8), with the extended definition of A, the determination of $\hat{\boldsymbol{d}}_T$ requires

$$p(\boldsymbol{\omega}_T \mid \boldsymbol{y}_T^o, \boldsymbol{d}_T, A) = \sum_{j=1}^{n} p(A_j \mid \boldsymbol{y}_T^o, A) p(\boldsymbol{\omega}_T \mid \boldsymbol{y}_T^o, \boldsymbol{d}_T, A_j). \quad (2.11)$$

The construction of $p(\boldsymbol{\omega}_T \mid \boldsymbol{y}_T^o, \boldsymbol{d}_T, A_j)$ follows precisely the first two steps in Bayesian inference described in section 2.1, A being replaced by A_j.

The other component of (2.11) is the posterior model probability

$$p(A_j \mid \boldsymbol{y}_T^o, A) = \frac{p(A_j \mid A) p(\boldsymbol{y}_T^o \mid A_j)}{\sum_{i=1}^{n} p(A_i \mid A) p(\boldsymbol{y}_T^o \mid A_i)}, \quad (2.12)$$

for each $j = 1, \dots, n$. It is determined by the model prior probability $p(A_j \mid A)$ and the marginal likelihood

$$p(\boldsymbol{y}_T^o \mid A_j) = \int_{\Theta_{A_j}} p(\boldsymbol{\theta}_{A_j,T} \mid A_j) p(\boldsymbol{y}_T^o \mid \boldsymbol{\theta}_{A_j,T}, A_j) \, \mathrm{d}\boldsymbol{\theta}_{A_j,T}. \quad (2.13)$$

It is through (2.13), and then (2.12) and (2.11), that the evidence $\boldsymbol{y}_T^o$ comes to bear in resolving conflicts $\hat{\boldsymbol{d}}_{T,i} \neq \hat{\boldsymbol{d}}_{T,j}$. In general, of course, it will not be the case that $\hat{\boldsymbol{d}}_T = \hat{\boldsymbol{d}}_{T,j}$ for any $j = 1, \dots, n$.

This combination of models depends critically on the assumption that $\boldsymbol{y}_T$ and $\boldsymbol{\omega}_T$ are not model specific, reflected in the notation set up in the previous section. This assumption seems unassailable in the case of $\boldsymbol{\omega}_T$, which is dictated by the decision maker's situation: a model A_j must address the distribution of $\boldsymbol{\omega}_T$ in order to be in the running. (Models for air traffic control are rather different than those supporting monetary policy.) The assumption that the observables are the same in each model is standard, but need not be true in practice.

2.3 Simulation

The Bayesian paradigm provides a complete and coherent approach to decision making. However, it takes many things as given. Two of these, the model A or models A_j, and the data $\boldsymbol{y}_T^o$, have already been noted. The difficulty here is in finding models and data that lead to satisfactory and reliable decisions $\hat{\boldsymbol{d}}_T$. By this it is meant that formal modeling leads to decisions improving on a naive or arbitrary decision $\boldsymbol{d}_T^0$, and to a reasonable evaluation of the consequences of those decisions. If the same decision were made repeatedly at $T = T_0, \dots, T_1$—for example in weather forecasting, more arguably in monetary policy, and certainly not in climate policy—one might begin to formalize "satisfactory and reliable decisions" along the lines of

$$\sum_{T=T_0}^{T_1} \mathrm{E}[U(\boldsymbol{\omega}_T, \hat{\boldsymbol{d}}_T) \mid \boldsymbol{y}_{T-1}^o, A] \approxeq \sum_{T=T_0}^{T_1} U(\boldsymbol{\omega}_T, \hat{\boldsymbol{d}}_T)$$
$$\gg \sum_{T=T_0}^{T_1} U(\boldsymbol{\omega}_T, \boldsymbol{d}_T^0).$$

This is largely beyond the scope of this monograph, although chapter 5 addresses some elements of this process.

Regardless of whether models are poor or excellent, or of the difficulty in obtaining data, the Bayesian paradigm also assumes the ability to carry out the many computations indicated in the previous two sections. For all but the simplest models, serious problems begin at (2.6) once it is noted that

$$p(\boldsymbol{\theta}_{A,T} \mid \boldsymbol{y}_T^o, A) = \frac{p(\boldsymbol{\theta}_{A,T} \mid A) p(\boldsymbol{y}_T^o \mid \boldsymbol{\theta}_{A,T}, A)}{\int p(\boldsymbol{\theta}_{A,T} \mid A) p(\boldsymbol{y}_T^o \mid \boldsymbol{\theta}_{A,T}, A) \, \mathrm{d}\boldsymbol{\theta}_{A,T}}.$$

The integral in the denominator is almost always analytically intractable. Independent of this problem (that is, even if one had a practical closed-form expression for $p(\boldsymbol{\theta}_{A,T} \mid \boldsymbol{y}_T^o, A)$), (2.7) demands another analytically intractable integration.

The joint problem can be solved if it is possible, first, to simulate the vector of unobservables $\boldsymbol{\theta}_{A,T}$ from the posterior density (2.6),

$$\boldsymbol{\theta}_{A,T}^{(m)} \mid (\boldsymbol{y}_T^o, A) \sim p(\boldsymbol{\theta}_{A,T} \mid \boldsymbol{y}_T^o, A) \quad (m = 1, 2, \dots), \tag{2.14}$$

and, second, to simulate the vector of interest $\boldsymbol{\omega}_T$ conditional on unobservables and data $\boldsymbol{y}_T^o$,

$$\boldsymbol{\omega}_T^{(m)} \mid (\boldsymbol{y}_T^o, \boldsymbol{\theta}_{A,T}, \boldsymbol{d}_T, A) \sim p(\boldsymbol{\omega}_T \mid \boldsymbol{y}_T^o, \boldsymbol{\theta}_{A,T}, \boldsymbol{d}_T). \tag{2.15}$$

By simulating $\boldsymbol{\theta}_{A,T}^{(m)} \mid (\boldsymbol{y}_T^o, A)$ from the marginal posterior distribution (2.14) and then drawing $\boldsymbol{\omega}_T^{(m)} \mid (\boldsymbol{y}_T^o, \boldsymbol{\theta}_{A,T}^{(m)}, A)$ from the conditional posterior distribution (2.15), it follows that

$$(\boldsymbol{\theta}_{A,T}^{(m)}, \boldsymbol{\omega}_T^{(m)}) \sim p(\boldsymbol{\theta}_{A,T}, \boldsymbol{\omega}_T \mid \boldsymbol{y}_T^o, \boldsymbol{d}_T, A).$$

Consequently,

$$\boldsymbol{\omega}_T^{(m)} \sim p(\boldsymbol{\omega}_T \mid \boldsymbol{y}_T^o, \boldsymbol{d}_T, A),$$

the density required at (2.7). Repeating (2.14) followed by (2.15) with $\boldsymbol{\theta}_{A,T} = \boldsymbol{\theta}_{A,T}^{(m)}$, appealing to (2.5) one can approximate $\hat{\boldsymbol{d}}_T$ if, third, it is possible to solve the optimization problem

$$\hat{\boldsymbol{d}}_T^{(M)} = \underset{\boldsymbol{d}_T}{\operatorname{argmax}} M^{-1} \sum_{m=1}^{M} U(\boldsymbol{\omega}_T^{(m)}, \boldsymbol{d}_T). \qquad (2.16)$$

If the Bayesian paradigm is to be implemented in this way, the simulations (2.14) and (2.15) must be practical, the optimization (2.16) must be feasible, and there must be some guarantee that $\hat{\boldsymbol{d}}_T^{(M)} \to \boldsymbol{d}_T$, ideally with probability 1 as $M \to \infty$.

Algorithms that implement (2.14), known collectively as posterior simulators, began to be developed for econometric models in the late 1980s.[2] The leading approaches, importance sampling and Markov chain Monte Carlo, both guarantee that simulation approximations to posterior moments converge with probability 1 under conditions that can be verified, and provide central limit theorems for assessing the accuracy of the approximation for a simulation sample of size M. Depending on the model, a posterior simulator can be sophisticated and intricate, and there is a large literature on the theory and implementation of these methods. Koop (2003), Lancaster (2004), Geweke (2005), and Rossi et al. (2005) all discuss posterior simulators in the context of econometric models. For many econometric models, public-domain software for (2.14) is readily available; for others, importance sampling or Markov chain Monte Carlo algorithms can be constructed that accomplish (2.14); and some models pose serious challenges for posterior simulation.

[2] Earlier simulation algorithms can be found in Zellner (1971, appendix C) and in Kloek and van Dijk (1978). They were inherently limited to models much simpler than those used in support of decision making at the time, to say nothing of models in use today.

This monograph does not assume any detailed knowledge of how these simulators work, or experience in using them.

The second simulation requirement (2.15) is often less demanding. For example, in a pure prediction problem with $\boldsymbol{\omega}_T' = (\tilde{\boldsymbol{y}}_{T+1}', \dots, \tilde{\boldsymbol{y}}_{T+f}')$, (2.4) leads to the recursions

$$\tilde{\boldsymbol{y}}_{T+j}^{(m)} \sim p(\tilde{\boldsymbol{y}}_{T+j} \mid \tilde{\boldsymbol{y}}_{T+j-1}^{(m)}, \dots, \tilde{\boldsymbol{y}}_{T+1}^{(m)}, \tilde{\boldsymbol{y}}_T^o, \dots, \tilde{\boldsymbol{y}}_1^o, \boldsymbol{\theta}_{A,T}^{(m)}, A)$$

for $j = 1, \dots, f$. Given the recursive construction of most models these simulations are often straightforward, whereas in the same circumstances it is more difficult to construct the posterior simulator (2.14). But in general, $p(\boldsymbol{\omega}_T \mid \boldsymbol{y}_T, \boldsymbol{\theta}_{A,T}, \boldsymbol{d}_T)$ need not bear any relation at all to $p(\boldsymbol{y}_T \mid \boldsymbol{\theta}_{A,T}, A)$. Indeed, it may not be possible to express this density in closed form, yet the simulation (2.15), while not immediate, is still feasible. Important cases are those in which $\boldsymbol{\omega}_T$ represents stochastic realizations conditional on an equilibrium, the equilibrium in turn being a function of $\boldsymbol{\theta}_{A,T}$. Simulation methods and the Bayesian paradigm have proved successful in these models: for example, dynamic stochastic general equilibrium models supporting central bank decision making, and models of cooperative equilibrium supporting antitrust regulatory decisions. In such complex models, uncertainty about parameters is usually a major contributor to uncertainty about $\boldsymbol{\omega}_T$. The posterior simulation literature directly addresses the situation in which $\boldsymbol{\omega}_T$ is a deterministic function of $\boldsymbol{\theta}_{A,T}$; Geweke (2005) shows that it is not hard to extend results on convergence in that literature to the more general case, here, that is relevant for decision making.

The final simulation requirement is solution of the optimization problem (2.16). If $\mathcal{D}$ includes only a few points, e.g., if the decision is whether or not to permit a proposed merger of two firms, with perhaps a few divestment conditions if the merger is approved, then optimization amounts only to simulation approximation of $\mathrm{E}[U(\boldsymbol{\omega}_T, \boldsymbol{d}_T) \mid \boldsymbol{y}_T^o, A]$ for the relevant values of $\boldsymbol{d}_T$. When $\boldsymbol{d}_T$ is continuous, (2.16) entails optimization of a simulated objective function. Geweke (2005) provides conditions under which

$$\hat{\boldsymbol{d}}_T^{(M)} \xrightarrow{\text{a.s.}} \boldsymbol{d}_T$$

and

$$M^{-1} \sum_{m=1}^{M} U(\boldsymbol{\omega}_T^{(m)}, \hat{\boldsymbol{d}}_T^{(M)}) \xrightarrow{\text{a.s.}} \mathrm{E}[U(\boldsymbol{\omega}_T, \hat{\boldsymbol{d}}_T)]$$

as $M \to \infty$, and methods for evaluating the accuracy of these approximations.

2.4 Model Evaluation

Prediction is central to Bayes's theorem and to the Bayesian paradigm. Evidence about unobservables is systematically updated by the probability of new evidence conditional on alternative values of the unobservables. In the case of a single model A,

$$\begin{aligned} p(\boldsymbol{\theta}_{A,T} \mid \boldsymbol{y}_T^o, A) &= k_T \cdot p(\boldsymbol{\theta}_{A,T} \mid A) p(\boldsymbol{y}_T^o \mid \boldsymbol{\theta}_{A,T}, A) \\ &= k_T \cdot p(\boldsymbol{\theta}_{A,T} \mid A) \prod_{t=1}^{T} p(\tilde{\boldsymbol{y}}_t^o \mid \boldsymbol{y}_{t-1}^o, \boldsymbol{\theta}_{A,T}, A), \end{aligned} \tag{2.17}$$

where

$$k_T = \left[\int_{\Theta_{A,T}} p(\boldsymbol{\theta}_{A,T} \mid A) p(\boldsymbol{y}_T^o \mid \boldsymbol{\theta}_{A,T}, A) \, \mathrm{d}\boldsymbol{\theta}_{A,T} \right]^{-1}$$

depends on $\boldsymbol{y}_T^o$ but not $\boldsymbol{\theta}_{A,T}$. The posterior density of $\boldsymbol{\theta}_{A,T}$ therefore embeds the one-step-ahead prediction record associated with alternative values of $\boldsymbol{\theta}_{A,T}$.[3] From (2.17),

$$p(\boldsymbol{\theta}_{A,T} \mid \boldsymbol{y}_T^o, A) \\ \propto p(\boldsymbol{\theta}_{A,T} \mid \boldsymbol{y}_{T-1}^o, A) p(\tilde{\boldsymbol{y}}_T^o \mid \boldsymbol{y}_{T-1}^o, \boldsymbol{\theta}_{A,T}, A).$$

In the case of multiple models $A = \{A_1, \dots, A_n\}$,

$$\begin{aligned} p(A_j \mid \boldsymbol{y}_T^o, A) &= k_T' \cdot p(A_j \mid A) p(\boldsymbol{y}_T^o \mid A_j) \\ &= k_T' \cdot p(A_j \mid \boldsymbol{y}_{T-1}^o, A) p(\tilde{\boldsymbol{y}}_T^o \mid \boldsymbol{y}_{T-1}^o, A_j), \end{aligned} \tag{2.18}$$

where

$$k_T' = \left[\sum_{i=1}^{n} p(A_i \mid A) p(\boldsymbol{y}_T^o \mid A_i) \right]^{-1}$$

depends on $\boldsymbol{y}_T^o$ but not A_j. The data affect model probabilities only through the probabilities that models assign to what is observed, a well-known consequence of the likelihood principle. Implicit in (2.18) is the comparison between models inherent in the posterior odds ratio,

$$\frac{p(A_i \mid \boldsymbol{y}_T^o, A)}{p(A_j \mid \boldsymbol{y}_T^o, A)} = \frac{p(A_i \mid A)}{p(A_j \mid A)} \cdot \frac{p(\boldsymbol{y}_T^o \mid A_i)}{p(\boldsymbol{y}_T^o \mid A_j)},$$

the product of the prior odds ratio and the Bayes factor for models A_i and A_j. The posterior odds ratio is

[3] There is nothing special about single-step prediction. Equation (2.17) can be expressed using multi-step densities as well.

systematically updated by the predictive Bayes factor:

$$\frac{p(A_i \mid \boldsymbol{y}_T^o, A)}{p(A_j \mid \boldsymbol{y}_T^o, A)} = \frac{p(A_i \mid \boldsymbol{y}_{T-1}^o, A)}{p(A_j \mid \boldsymbol{y}_{T-1}^o, A)} \cdot \frac{p(\tilde{\boldsymbol{y}}_T^o \mid \boldsymbol{y}_{T-1}^o, A_i)}{p(\tilde{\boldsymbol{y}}_T^o \mid \boldsymbol{y}_{T-1}^o, A_j)}.$$

These interpretations of the evidence about models are all limited by the portfolio of models $A = \{A_1, \dots, A_n\}$ under consideration. Explicit in the notation in this chapter is that all statements are conditional on this portfolio. None of this analysis addresses the comparison of models with an absolute standard: the analysis applies in the same way whether the performances of the best models in the portfolio are considered excellent or are found to be deficient, assessed against this standard. On the other hand, decision makers care about the performance of models. For example, a model A provides not only $\hat{\boldsymbol{d}}_T$ but also $\mathrm{E}[U(\boldsymbol{\omega}_T, \hat{\boldsymbol{d}}_T) \mid \boldsymbol{y}_T^o, A]$; so long as $U(\boldsymbol{\omega}_T, \hat{\boldsymbol{d}}_T)$ can be evaluated, systematic inconsistencies between utility ex post and its expectation ex ante will surely be noticed.

The idea that models should be evaluated according to the consistency of their predictions with actual outcomes is central to science and to statistics. Procedures for rejecting models that are inconsistent with evidence are well-established in non-Bayesian statistics, although of course rejecting all models in a portfolio is hardly constructive from the perspective of the decision maker. Bayesian statisticians have developed two approaches to model evaluation, both based on comparing predictive distributions with actual outcomes. Both are well-suited to the simulation methods used to uncover these distributions described in the previous section.

2.4.1 Prior Predictive Analysis

The first two components of a complete model A_j imply a predictive density of observables; that is, the distribution of the data ex ante:

$$p(\boldsymbol{y}_T \mid A_j) = \int p(\boldsymbol{\theta}_{A_j,T} \mid A_j) p(\boldsymbol{y}_T \mid \boldsymbol{\theta}_{A_j,T}, A_j) \, \mathrm{d}\boldsymbol{\theta}_{A_j,T}. \tag{2.19}$$

The density (2.19) is the prior predictive density of the observables. It is the model's prediction of what might be observed prior to collecting data $\boldsymbol{y}_T^o$. Evaluating (2.19) ex post at the data point $\boldsymbol{y}_T = \boldsymbol{y}_T^o$ leads to the marginal likelihood (2.13). The weight of the evidence in determining the probability of the model in the portfolio is mediated entirely through $p(\boldsymbol{y}_T^o \mid A_j)$, as indicated in (2.12): it is the prior predictive density evaluated at the realized observation.

It is generally straightforward to access $p(\boldsymbol{y}_T \mid A_j)$ by simulation:

$$\boldsymbol{\theta}_{A_j,T}^{(m)} \sim p(\boldsymbol{\theta}_{A_j,T} \mid A_j), \qquad \boldsymbol{y}_T^{(m)} \sim p(\boldsymbol{y}_T \mid \boldsymbol{\theta}_{A_j,T}^{(m)}, A_j) \tag{2.20}$$

produces

$$(\boldsymbol{y}_T^{(m)}, \boldsymbol{\theta}_{A_j,T}^{(m)}) \sim p(\boldsymbol{\theta}_{A_j,T}, \boldsymbol{y}_T \mid A_j)$$

and consequently

$$\boldsymbol{y}_T^{(m)} \sim p(\boldsymbol{y}_T \mid A_j).$$

If the length j_T of the vector $\boldsymbol{y}_T$ were small, one could use these simulations directly to gain some understanding of the implications of the model for observables, and could use conventional smoothing methods to evaluate the marginal likelihood $p(\boldsymbol{y}_T^o \mid A_j)$. In practice, j_T is usually much too large to proceed in this way.

Implicit in (2.19) is the prior predictive density $p(\boldsymbol{z}_T \mid A_j)$ of any function of the observables $\boldsymbol{z}_T = h(\boldsymbol{y}_T)$. When h is chosen to define salient aspects of the observables, this distribution can be informative and useful. For example, in a macroeconomic model, h could provide the number of business cycles in a given time period, or the sample contemporaneous correlation between key observables like output, inflation, and interest rates; in an asset pricing model, h might indicate higher sample moments of returns or the range of returns over a given number of years; in a microeconomic model constructed to support a regulatory decision, h could compare pre- and post-merger prices.

Analytical expressions for the prior distribution of $\boldsymbol{z}_T = h(\boldsymbol{y}_T)$ are generally unavailable even when $p(\boldsymbol{\theta}_{A,T} \mid A)$ comes from a simple and well-known family. By comparison, it is usually straightforward to write computer code that maps $\boldsymbol{y}_T$ into $\boldsymbol{z}_T$, as the examples in the previous paragraph suggest. Given

$$\boldsymbol{y}_T^{(m)} \sim p(\boldsymbol{y}_T \mid A_j) \quad (m = 1, 2, \dots),$$

the collection $\boldsymbol{z}_T^{(m)} = h(\boldsymbol{y}_T^{(m)})$ $(m = 1, 2, \dots)$ is a simulation from the prior predictive density $p(\boldsymbol{z}_T \mid A)$; and, of course, $\boldsymbol{z}_T^o = h(\boldsymbol{y}_T^o)$ is the observed value of $\boldsymbol{z}_T$. These simulations can be very useful, in two related contexts.

One important application of prior predictive distributions is in model evaluation (as distinct from model comparison). This idea dates at least to Box (1980), who referred to h as a "relevant model checking function," and traces its use in this fashion to Good (1956) and Roberts (1965), among others. In Box's predictive checks one determines $\alpha_{\text{pre}} = P(z_T > z_T^o \mid A)$, which is tantamount to evaluating the prior c.d.f. of z_T at the observed value z_T^o. Given a prior simulation sample $z_T^{(m)}$ $(m = 1, \ldots, M)$, the simulation-consistent approximation of α_{pre} is

$$M^{-1} \sum_{m=1}^{M} I_{(z_T^o, \infty)}(z_T^o).$$

If α_{pre} is near 0, or near 1, then, in Box's language, the model A is discredited by the predictive check. Of course, such checks can be undertaken using any number of alternative functions h.

Example 2.1. Consider the simple model

$$y_t \overset{\text{i.i.d.}}{\sim} N(\mu, 1), \quad \mu \mid A \sim N(0, \underline{h}^{-1}),$$

$\underline{h}$ being the hyperparameter of $p(\mu \mid A)$ chosen by the investigator. Suppose the checking function is

$$\bar{y}_T = h(\boldsymbol{y}_T) = T^{-1} \sum_{t=1}^{T} y_t = \bar{y}_T.$$

The prior predictive distribution is $\bar{y}_T \sim N(0, \underline{h}^{-1} + T^{-1})$ and

$$\alpha_{\text{pre}} = \Phi[-\bar{y}_T^o(\underline{h}T)^{1/2}(\underline{h} + T)^{-1/2}]. \tag{2.21}$$

If the checking function is

$$z_T = h(\boldsymbol{y}_T) = \sum_{t=1}^{T} (y_t - \bar{y}_T)^2 = s_T^2,$$

then the prior predictive distribution is $s_T^2 \sim \chi^2(T-1)$. In this simple example the roles of the two checking functions are unambiguous. Since $\bar{y}_T$ is a sufficient statistic, it provides evidence on the implications of $p(\mu \mid A)$. Since s_T^2 is an ancillary statistic, it provides information on the implications of $p(\boldsymbol{y}_T \mid \mu, A)$.

Box's prior predictive checks have several attractions. One is that the logical foundations of the prior predictive distribution are transparent and unambiguous, unlike the alternative discussed in section 2.4.2. Another is that checking functions h may be a useful device for communicating information about model inadequacy to the decision maker. On the other hand, the decision whether to discredit the model based on prior c.d.f. evaluation at z_T^o violates the likelihood principle. "Prior predictive p-values" are subject to the same difficulties as frequentist p-values documented in the Bayesian literature. Chapter 3 returns to this issue.

The related important application of prior predictive distributions arises in model creation and model improvement, where it provides strategic advantages for a research program. Compared with the design, checking, and application of posterior simulators, and perhaps the collection of data appropriate to the model, prior predictive analysis is often fast and cheap. Simulating

$$\boldsymbol{\theta}_{A,T}^{(m)} \sim p(\boldsymbol{\theta}_{A,T} \mid A)$$

followed by

$$\boldsymbol{y}_T^{(m)} \sim p(\boldsymbol{y}_T \mid \boldsymbol{\theta}_{A,T}^{(m)}, A)$$

and

$$\boldsymbol{z}_T^{(m)} = h(\boldsymbol{y}_T^{(m)})$$

can sometimes be done in an afternoon, whereas carrying through to a posterior distribution with appropriate data might require weeks or months.[4] The prior

[4] The same can often be said for non-Bayesian methods of inference, including (pseudo-) maximum likelihood and the generalized method of moments. Prior predictive analysis can be useful for non-Bayesians, too.

predictive exercise can indicate that a model is incapable of accounting for important observed characteristics of data: so-called stylized facts. The exercise typically involves experimentation with $p(\boldsymbol{\theta}_{A,T} \mid A)$ and often tinkering with $p(\boldsymbol{y}_T \mid \boldsymbol{\theta}_{A,T}, A)$, both of which are likely to increase the econometrician's understanding of the model. This understanding can be critical to the interpretation of findings, should the research proceed to formal posterior inference, and it is often useful in thinking about alternative models, should the researcher decide to abandon model A.

Prior predictive analysis is a specific instance of model specification analysis, a well-established part of good applied econometric practice. It places specification analysis ahead of formal inference, unlike virtually all non-Bayesian specification analysis, which is based on a fitted model (see, for example, Hendry 1995). This is rooted in the fact that a complete model provides a full predictive distribution of observables and any function of observables. The completeness is essential: in particular, if there is no proper prior distribution, then the exercise is impossible. This provides the logical foundation for specification analysis preceding inference. Simulation methods make it relatively fast and cheap.

2.4.2 Posterior Predictive Analysis

Yet prior predictive analysis is clearly no substitute for posterior inference. Moreover, if the data are informative, so that the posterior distribution of $\boldsymbol{\theta}_{A,T}$ is much more concentrated than the prior distribution, then the posterior may reveal that the model A cannot account well for all elements of $\boldsymbol{z}_T^o$ simultaneously. This insight underlies posterior predictive analysis.

The mechanics of posterior predictive analysis are straightforward. Given a posterior simulation sample $\{\boldsymbol{\theta}_{A,T}^{(m)}\}$ from (2.14), construct a corresponding draw

$$\boldsymbol{y}_T^{(m)} \sim p(\boldsymbol{y}_T \mid \boldsymbol{\theta}_{A,T}^{(m)}, A)$$

along with $\boldsymbol{z}_T^{(m)} = h(\boldsymbol{y}_T^{(m)})$. If $\boldsymbol{z}_T^o$ lies far from the bulk of the distribution of $\{\boldsymbol{z}_T^{(m)}\}$, then there is a problem with the model. For univariate z_T one can evaluate the posterior c.d.f. at the point z_T^o and interpret values near 0 or 1 as discrediting the model, as Box did with the prior predictive distribution.

Some reflection on this procedure reveals that it amounts to predicting the distribution of $\boldsymbol{z}_T$ in a repetition of the "experiment" that produced $\boldsymbol{y}_T^o$, with the specification that the experiment will be carried out with model A and the same values of the unobservables $\boldsymbol{\theta}_{A,T}$. Careful expositions of posterior predictive analysis, for example Gelman et al. (1996), are explicit about this interpretation. To emphasize the interpretation, let $\tilde{\boldsymbol{z}}_T$ denote the random vector drawn from the posterior predictive distribution (Gelman et al. use the notation $\boldsymbol{z}_T^{\text{rep}}$). The common sense appears unassailable: if the model predicts that something very different would happen in a repetition of the experiment, one should be suspicious of the model. Stated another way, if the model predicts that in repetitions of the experiment one would almost never observe an important discrete event that occurred in the initial experiment—the one carried out in the real world—then something is wrong. Computing the "significance level" α_{post} of z_T^o from the output of the posterior simulator formalizes this idea.

This is a violation of the likelihood principle that many Bayesians regard as egregious: rendering a negative conclusion about a model based on events that did not happen and were assigned very low posterior probability—that is, the remaining tail of the posterior predictive distribution. A more subtle difficulty comes from the identification of a repetition of the experiment, informed by the sample, with features of that same sample—a form of overfitting.

Example 2.2. Returning to the situation of example 2.1, the posterior predictive distribution is

$$N\left[\frac{T\bar{y}_T^o}{\underline{h}+T}, \frac{\underline{h}+2T}{T(\underline{h}+T)}\right].$$

Evaluating the c.d.f. of this distribution at the observed value $\bar{y}_T^o$ leads to

$$\alpha_{\text{post}} = \Phi\left[\frac{-T^{1/2}\underline{h}\bar{y}_T^o}{(\underline{h}+2T)^{1/2}(\underline{h}+T)^{1/2}}\right]. \tag{2.22}$$

Referring to (2.21) let $w = -\bar{y}_T^o(\underline{h}T)^{1/2}(\underline{h}+T)^{-1/2}$, and then, from (2.22),

$$\alpha_{\text{post}} = \Phi\left[w\left(\frac{r}{2+r}\right)^{1/2}\right], \quad r = \underline{h}/T.$$

Figure 2.1 shows the relation between α_{pre} and α_{post} as a function of r, the ratio of prior to sample precision. Because $[r/(2+r)]^{1/2} < 1$, it is always the case that $|\alpha_{\text{post}} - 0.5| < |\alpha_{\text{pre}} - 0.5|$. For the typical situation in which $\underline{h} \ll T$, $\alpha_{\text{post}} \approxeq 0.5$ when $\alpha_{\text{pre}} \in (0.001, 0.1)$. If prior and posterior predictive analyses use tail probabilities to criticize this model, as suggested by Box (1980) and Gelman et al. (1996), then the prior predictive analysis will provide more evidence against the model than will the posterior predictive analysis.

The posterior predictive distribution of the ancillary statistic s_T^2 is (tautologically) the same as the prior distribution. Therefore, prior and posterior predictive

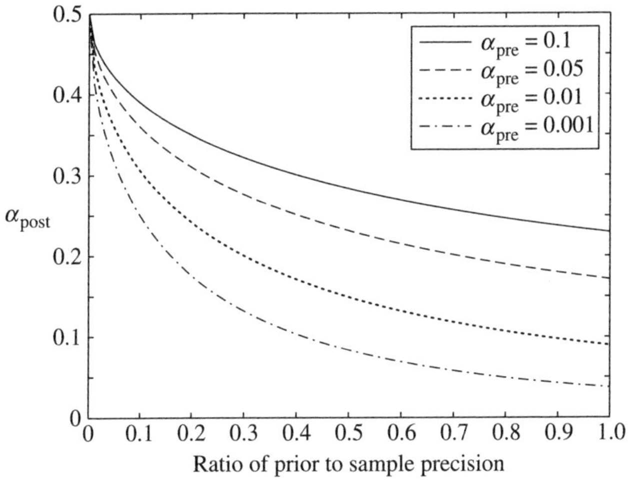

Figure 2.1. The relationship between α_{pre} (2.21) and α_{post} (2.22).

analysis will lead to the same information about the credibility of the model.

Example 2.2 raises another difficulty with using α_{post} for model criticism. For the single sufficient statistic in that example $|\alpha_{\mathrm{post}} - 0.5| < |\alpha_{\mathrm{pre}} - 0.5|$, whereas for any ancillary statistic in any model $\alpha_{\mathrm{post}} = \alpha_{\mathrm{pre}}$. Models that provide credible support for actual decisions are sufficiently complex that there is rarely a known sufficient statistic other than the sample $\boldsymbol{y}_T^o$ itself. Checking functions $h(\boldsymbol{y}_t)$ in such models cannot be characterized neatly as sufficient or ancillary, but the examples in this section raise serious questions about the efficacy of posterior predictive analysis. The next chapter returns to this issue.

3

Prior Predictive Analysis and Model Evaluation

Prior predictive analysis, described in section 2.4.1, is a versatile tool that provides insight into the characteristics of a model and the means to evaluate a model's adequacy for given data. This chapter illustrates prior predictive analysis and introduces two new techniques: one for studying model characteristics and the other for model evaluation. The emphasis is on the serious application of subjective Bayesian methods, and therefore all of the methods used are consistent with the likelihood principle.

The illustration involves a well-used data set: the monthly Standard & Poor's (S&P) 500 return series. The models considered here are comparatively simple and well-understood: the i.i.d. Gaussian model, the generalized autoregressive conditional heteroscedasticity (GARCH) model, and the stochastic volatility (SV) model. The intention is to introduce and illustrate methods in familiar empirical territory, not to break fresh ground with new data or models. Section 3.1 presents the data and models.

The following section begins by undertaking a conventional prior predictive analysis along the lines discussed in section 2.4.1 using several checking functions. This analysis provides some indications of the capabilities and shortfalls of these models. Many of these are well-understood, others less so; those in the former category illustrate how known problems with models become manifest in prior predictive analysis. Section 3.2 closes by introducing an analysis of variance for prior predictive distributions. Motivated by the concerns about posterior predictive analysis discussed in section 2.4.2, this analysis leads to a measure of ancillarity.

The final section of this chapter provides a practical Bayesian alternative to conventional model evaluation based on tail probabilities described by Box (1980) and Gelman et al. (1996), denoted by α_{pre} and α_{post} in section 2.4. It extends ideas introduced in Geweke (2007) and illustrates them using the data and models documented in section 3.1. Systematic application of this procedure requires evaluation of multidimensional distributions, and section 3.3 shows how this can be accomplished with Gaussian copulas.

3.1 Data and Models

The data and models used in this chapter are among the most familiar in the financial econometrics literature.

3.1.1 Data

The data set is the S&P 500 index at the end of the month (adjusted for reinvestment of dividends) for 1926:1 through 2007:12 from Wharton Research Data Services. Figure 3.1 shows the natural logarithm of this series and also identifies some months used subsequently in section 3.2.1 in defining features of interest in the data. A bear market begins the first time the

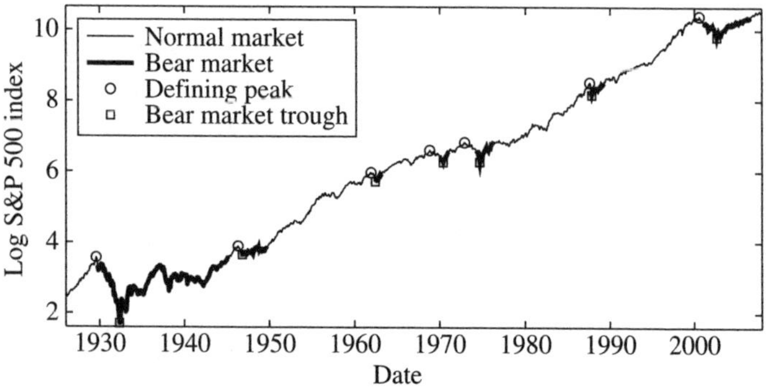

Figure 3.1. Log U.S. S&P 500 index, dividends reinvested.

index falls 20% or more below its previous peak and ends when it first attains or exceeds the level of the previous peak. In figure 3.1 the index is plotted with a thicker line during bear markets. The peaks defining these markets are indicated by circles and the squares show the trough of each bear market. The bear market of the Great Depression stands out for its length and depth.

The S&P 500 return series, denoted by $\{y_t\}$ in this chapter, is the first difference of the one plotted in figure 3.1 and is shown in figure 3.2 as the lighter and more volatile line. The thicker line provides a thirteen-month centered moving average of the monthly returns. Visual inspection of the return series itself does not suggest autocorrelation in returns, and the same inspection of the moving average does not suggest autocorrelation at intervals greater than a year. (Of course, casual inspection of this kind is notoriously unreliable compared with the more exacting analysis pursued in section 3.2.2 or that using conventional tests.)

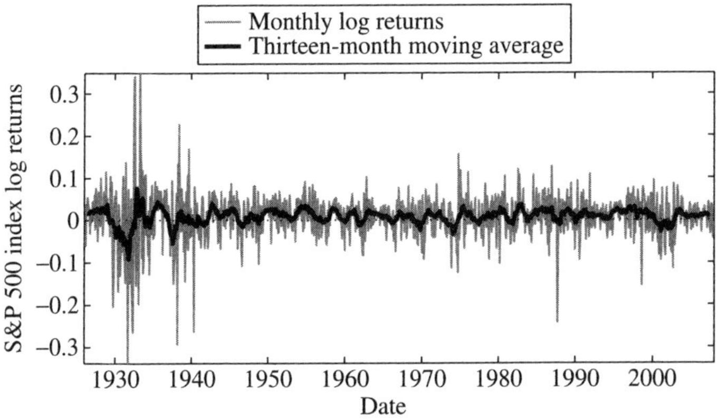

Figure 3.2. U.S. S&P 500 index log returns, dividends reinvested.

Yet figure 3.2 strongly suggests that returns are not independent. Even more directly it suggests that returns do not satisfy the condition of exchangeability: if one were to randomly permute the return series, its appearance would change dramatically (and in fact it is a trivial matter to write computer code that does this). The most prominent departure from independence is the apparent persistence in volatility. This is clearer in figure 3.3, in which the thick line is constructed in the same way as for figure 3.2 except that it begins with the absolute return series. The thirteen-month moving average in figure 3.3 appears to show serial correlation well beyond one year. Even more dramatic is the secular decrease in volatility from the early 1930s through the end of the sample.[1]

[1] Inclusion of 2008 returns would change the end of the time series dramatically. At the time of writing in early 2009 returns adjusted for reinvestment of dividends were not yet available for 2008.

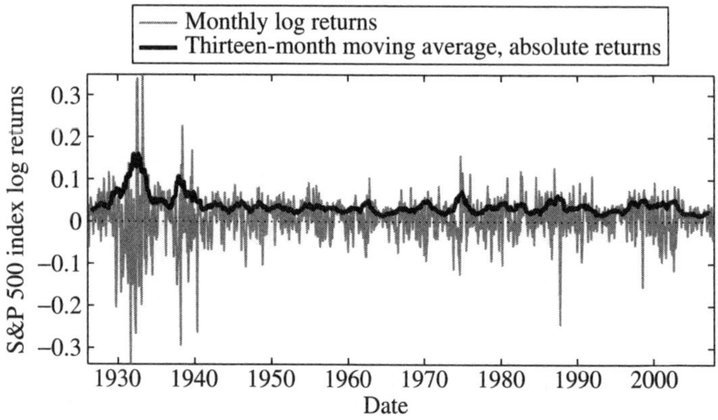

Figure 3.3. U.S. S&P 500 index log returns, dividends reinvested.

3.1.2 A Gaussian Model

The first of the three models studied is one of the simplest and best understood:

$$y_t \overset{\text{i.i.d.}}{\sim} N(\mu, \sigma^2).$$

Its deficiencies as a model of returns have long been recognized. Many of these are evident in figures 3.2 and 3.3 and they are well-known in financial econometrics. The model is included here for readers who understand the problems with the model but are less familiar with prior predictive analysis: section 3.2 shows how these problems are revealed in the analysis.

Working toward a complete model, the prior distribution has two independent components. A Gaussian prior for μ is conditionally conjugate for μ, as is an inverted gamma prior for σ^2. The analysis that follows uses the independent priors

$$\mu \sim N(0.008, 0.003^2) \tag{3.1}$$

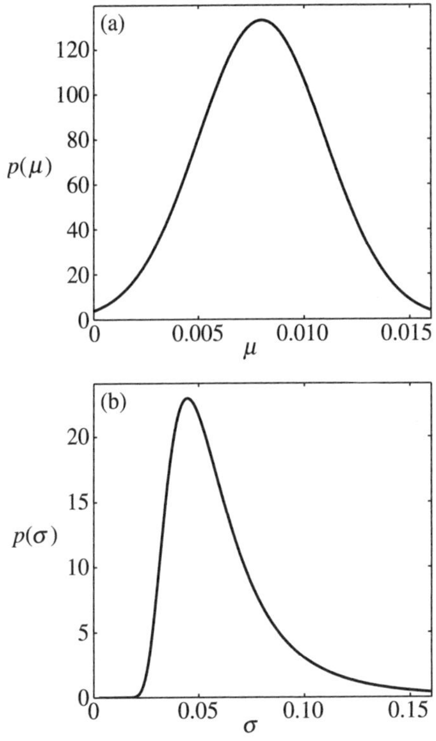

Figure 3.4. Prior densities of (a) μ and (b) σ, all three models.

and

$$\frac{0.01}{\sigma^2} \sim \chi^2(4) \iff \frac{1}{\sigma^2} \sim \text{Gamma}(2, 200). \qquad (3.2)$$

Figure 3.4 shows the prior densities for μ and σ. These prior densities will be retained for the population mean and standard deviation in the GARCH and SV models as well.

Because the Gaussian model has only location and scale parameters, many population properties appear to be inconsistent with the S&P 500 returns series. For example, $\text{cov}[(y_t - \mu)^2, (y_{t-s} - \mu)^2] = 0$ for all $s \neq 0$, which appears to be inconsistent with the behavior displayed in figure 3.3, and it will be seen that the corresponding sample moment appears to conflict with this restriction as well. Similarly, population excess kurtosis is identically zero, whereas sample information suggests otherwise. Of course such casual comparisons of sample and population moments do not tell us much, and can even be misleading. Section 3.2.2 and chapter 4 return to this issue.

3.1.3 A GARCH Model

The generalized autoregressive conditional heteroscedasticity (1,1) (hereafter, simply GARCH) model may be expressed

$$y_t \sim N(\mu, \sigma_t^2), \qquad \sigma_t^2 = \alpha_0 + \alpha_1 \varepsilon_{t-1}^2 + \beta_1 \sigma_{t-1}^2,$$

with

$$\alpha_0 > 0, \qquad \alpha_1 \geqslant 0, \qquad \beta_1 \geqslant 0. \tag{3.3}$$

Clearly, $\text{E}(y_t) = \mu$. Bollerslev (1986, 1988) and He and Terasvirta (1999) establish additional unconditional moments, as follows.

(1) If, in addition to (3.3),

$$\alpha_1 + \beta_1 < 1, \tag{3.4}$$

then the unconditional variance

$$\sigma^2 = \frac{\alpha_0}{1 - \alpha_1 - \beta_1} \tag{3.5}$$

exists.

(2) If, in addition to (3.3),

$$\beta_1^2 + 2\alpha_1\beta_1 + 3\alpha_1^2 < 1, \tag{3.6}$$

then the fourth moment exists and in this case the unconditional excess kurtosis is

$$\kappa = \frac{6\alpha_1^2}{1 - \beta_1^2 - 2\alpha_1\beta_1 - 3\alpha_1^2} \geqslant 0. \tag{3.7}$$

(3) Given the inequality (3.6), the first-order autocorrelation of squared deviations from the mean is

$$\begin{aligned} \rho &= \operatorname{corr}[(y_t - \mu)^2, (y_{t-1} - \mu)^2] \\ &= \frac{\alpha_1(1 - \beta_1^2 - \alpha_1\beta_1)}{1 - \beta_1^2 - 2\alpha_1\beta_1} \geqslant 0. \end{aligned} \tag{3.8}$$

These relationships impose two constraints on the set of population moments (ρ, κ) consistent with any GARCH model. The first constraint arises from (3.3), (3.7), and (3.8). From (3.7), $\partial\kappa/\partial\beta_1 \geqslant 0$, and from (3.8), $\partial\rho/\partial\beta_1 \leqslant 0$. If $\beta_1 = 0$ then, from (3.7) and (3.8), $\kappa = 6\rho^2/(1 - 3\rho^2)$, a relationship imposed in the ARCH(1) model. Consequently, due to the nonnegativity constraint on β_1 in (3.3), $\kappa \geqslant 6\rho^2/(1 - 3\rho^2)$; equivalently,

$$\rho \leqslant [\kappa/(6 + 3\kappa)]^{1/2} < 3^{-1/2}. \tag{3.9}$$

The second constraint arises from (3.4), (3.7), and (3.8):

$$\begin{aligned} 1 - \beta_1 > \alpha_1 &\iff 1 - \beta_1^2 > \alpha_1 + \alpha_1\beta_1 \\ &\iff 1 - \beta_1^2 - \alpha_1\beta_1 > \alpha_1 \\ &\iff 6\alpha_1(1 - \beta_1^2 - \alpha_1\beta_1) > 6\alpha_1^2 \\ &\iff 6(1 - \beta_1^2 - 2\alpha_1\beta_1)\rho > 6\alpha_1^2 \\ &\iff 3(\kappa + 2)\rho > \kappa \\ &\iff \rho > \frac{\kappa}{3(\kappa + 2)}. \end{aligned} \tag{3.10}$$

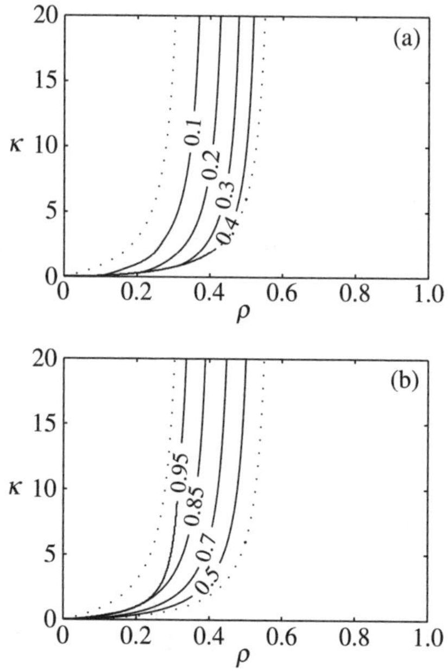

Figure 3.5. Some aspects of the prior distribution in the GARCH model. (a) α_1 as a function of ρ and κ. (b) β_1 as a function of ρ and κ.

Panels (a) and (b) of figure 3.5 show the range of (ρ, κ) combinations permitted in the GARCH model and their relation to the parameters α_1 and β_1. The dotted line on the right reflects the first constraint in (3.9) and the dotted line on the left reflects the constraint (3.10). Values of α_1 close to the lower bound $\alpha_1 = 0$ combined with values of β_1 near the upper bound $\beta_1 = 1$ account for many more of the (ρ, κ) combinations than do values of α_1 close to $3^{-1/2}$ and values of β_1 close to 0. It is clear, from these two panels, that a prior distribution taking α_1 uniform on $[0, 3^{-1/2})$ and β_1 uniform on $[0, 1)$, subject to (3.4)

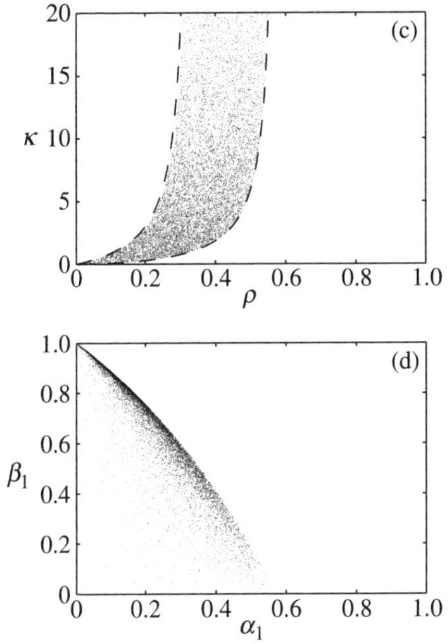

Figure 3.5. (*Continued.*) (c) Prior distribution of ρ and κ. (d) Prior distribution of α_1 and β_1.

and (3.6), would induce a prior distribution on ρ, κ concentrated near the right boundary of (ρ, κ) combinations, which are those arising in the ARCH(1) model.

Rather than express a prior distribution directly for the four parameters of the model, one can begin by placing prior distributions on the four population moments μ, σ, ρ, and κ and then work backward to the prior distributions for $\boldsymbol{\theta}' = (\mu, \alpha_0, \alpha_1, \beta_1)'$. Since prior predictive analysis is carried out by simulation it is not necessary to solve analytically for the prior on $\boldsymbol{\theta}$. Moreover, it is easier to think about prior distributions for population moments, which may reasonably be regarded as independent, than it is to state a prior distribution for individual parameters, for which independence is unreasonable. Proceeding in this way also makes it possible to maintain the same substantive priors across very different models, and section 3.1.4 does just this.

This requires that (3.7) and (3.8) be solved for α_1 and β_1. There is no closed-form solution. These equations suggest several iterative algorithms for determining the roots. Of these, the choice

$$\left.\begin{aligned} \alpha &= (2\beta)^{-1}\{1 + 2\rho\beta - \beta^2 \\ &\qquad \pm [(\beta^2 - 2\rho\beta - 1)^2 - 4\beta\rho(1-\beta^2)]^{1/2}\}, \\ \beta &= (2\kappa)^{-1}\{-2\alpha\kappa + [4\kappa^2 - 8\alpha^2\kappa^2 - 24\kappa\alpha^2]^{1/2}\} \end{aligned}\right\} \tag{3.11}$$

guarantees convergence to the solution. Of the two solutions for α in (3.11), one satisfies (3.6) and the other does not.

The analysis that follows in section 3.2.2 employs an exponential prior distribution with mean 8 for κ and uniform $(0, 1)$ prior distribution for ρ, independent except that the support of (ρ, κ) is restricted as indicated in figure 3.5. The prior distributions for μ and σ are given by (3.1) and (3.2), respectively. The random variables μ, σ, and (ρ, κ) are mutually independent in the prior distribution. Figure 3.5(c) is a scatterplot of 10,000 random draws from the prior distribution of (ρ, κ). Mapping these draws into (α_1, β_1), using the functions portrayed in panels (a) and (b) of the figure, yields the scatterplot in panel (d). As panels (a) and (b) suggested would be the case, the prior distribution is heavily concentrated near the boundary (3.6).

3.1.4 A Stochastic Volatility Model

The SV model of Jacquier et al. (1994) may be expressed

$$
\begin{aligned}
y_t &\sim N(\mu, \sigma_t^2), \\
\log \sigma_t^2 &= \alpha + \delta \log \sigma_{t-1}^2 + \sigma_v v_t, \\
v_t &\overset{\text{i.i.d.}}{\sim} N(0, 1),
\end{aligned}
$$

with

$$\delta \in (-1, 1), \quad \sigma_v > 0. \tag{3.12}$$

As in the previous two models, $\mathrm{E}(y_t) = \mu$. Jacquier et al. (1994) provide the unconditional moments σ^2, ρ, and κ defined in section 3.1.3.

(1) The unconditional variance is

$$\sigma^2 = \mathrm{E}(\varepsilon_t^2) = \exp\left[\frac{\alpha}{1-\delta} + \frac{\sigma_v^2}{2(1-\delta^2)}\right]. \tag{3.13}$$

(2) The first-order autocorrelation of squared deviations from the mean is

$$
\begin{aligned}
\rho &= \mathrm{corr}[(y_t - \mu)^2, (y_{t-1} - \mu)^2] \\
&= \left[\exp\left(\frac{\delta\sigma_v^2}{1-\delta^2}\right) - 1\right] \Big/ \left[3\exp\left(\frac{\sigma_v^2}{1-\delta^2}\right) - 1\right].
\end{aligned} \tag{3.14}
$$

(3) The unconditional excess kurtosis is

$$\kappa = 3\exp\left(\frac{\sigma_v^2}{1-\delta^2}\right) - 3 > 0. \tag{3.15}$$

No additional constraints beyond those required for stationarity (3.12) are needed for existence of these population moments.

One can begin as in section 3.1.3 by placing prior distributions on the four population moments μ, σ,

ρ, and κ, and then determine the prior distributions implied for $\boldsymbol{\theta}' = (\mu, \delta, \alpha, \sigma_v)'$. Motivated by (3.15) define

$$q = \log\left(\frac{\kappa + 3}{3}\right) = \frac{\sigma_v^2}{1 - \delta^2} \tag{3.16}$$

and substitute (3.16) into (3.13) to get

$$\log(\sigma^2) = \frac{\alpha}{1 - \delta} + \frac{q}{2} \tag{3.17}$$

and into (3.14) to produce

$$\rho \cdot [3\exp(q) - 1] = \exp(\delta q) - 1. \tag{3.18}$$

The recursive solution is therefore

(1) from (3.18),

$$\delta = \frac{1}{q}\log\{\rho[3\exp(q) - 1] + 1\};$$

(2) from (3.16),

$$\sigma_v^2 = (1 - \delta^2)q;$$

(3) from (3.17),

$$\alpha = (1 - \delta)(\log\sigma^2 - \tfrac{1}{2}q). \tag{3.19}$$

The model places constraints on ρ and κ. From (3.15), $\exp[\sigma_v^2/(1 - \delta^2)] = (\kappa + 3)/3$. Substituting in (3.14) yields

$$\rho = \frac{[(\kappa + 3)/3]^{\delta} - 1}{\kappa + 2}.$$

This is a monotone increasing function of δ, and taking the limits as $\delta \to -1$ and $\delta \to 1$ shows that

$$\rho \in \left(\frac{-\kappa}{(\kappa + 2)(\kappa + 3)}, \frac{\kappa}{3(\kappa + 2)}\right). \tag{3.20}$$

The lower limit is irrelevant given that the prior distribution support for ρ is $[0, 1)$. The upper limit imposes constraints on (ρ, κ). The constraints are indicated by the dotted curves in panels (a) and (b) of figure 3.6, which provide (δ, σ_v) as a function of (ρ, κ). The upper limit on ρ in (3.20) is exactly the same as the lower limit on ρ in (3.10) imposed by the GARCH model.

Simulating from this prior amounts to drawing κ from the exponential prior and ρ from the uniform prior, but rejecting (κ, ρ) if (3.20) is violated. Then μ is drawn from (3.1) and σ^2 is drawn from (3.2). Figure 3.6(c) is a scatterplot of 10,000 random draws from the prior distribution of (ρ, κ). Mapping these draws into (δ, σ_v), using the functions portrayed in parts (a) and (b) of the figure, yields the scatterplot in part (d). The points there constitute 10,000 random draws from $p(\delta, \sigma_v)$. The corresponding draws for α are provided by (3.19).

3.2 Prior Predictive Analysis

The three complete models lead to prior predictive densities $p(\boldsymbol{y}_T \mid A_j)$ $(j = 1, 2, 3)$. For the sample described in section 3.1, $T = 983$. The prior predictive distributions are accessed by simulation as described in section 2.4.1. From (2.20),

$$\boldsymbol{\theta}_{A_j}^{(m)} \sim p(\boldsymbol{\theta}_{A_j} \mid A_j), \quad \boldsymbol{y}_T^{(m)} \sim p(\boldsymbol{y}_T \mid \boldsymbol{\theta}_{A_j}^{(m)}, A_j) \quad (m = 1, \dots, M) \quad (3.21)$$

produces

$$\boldsymbol{y}_T^{(m)} \sim p(\boldsymbol{y}_T \mid A_j) \quad (m = 1, \dots, M),$$

and then

$$\boldsymbol{z}_T^{(m)} = h(\boldsymbol{y}_T^{(m)}) \sim p(\boldsymbol{z}_T \mid A_j). \quad (3.22)$$

Section 3.2.1 presents functions h producing features that are the elements of $\boldsymbol{z}_T$, and a conventional prior

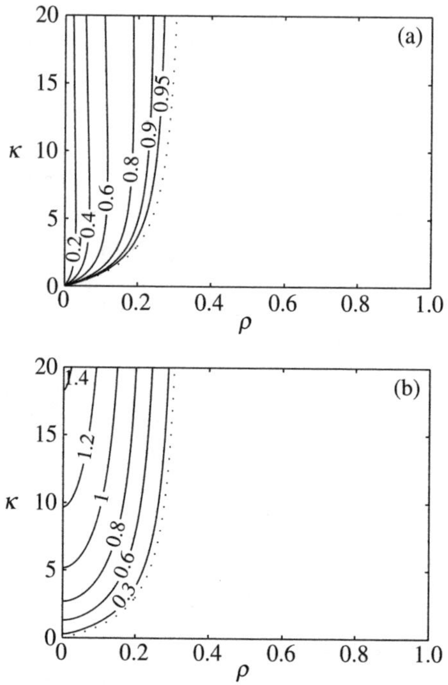

Figure 3.6. Some aspects of the prior distribution in the stochastic volatility model. (a) δ as a function of ρ and κ. (b) σ_v as a function of ρ and κ.

predictive analysis with these features is presented in section 3.2.2. Section 3.2.3 decomposes variation in $z_T \sim p(z_T \mid A)$ into two components, one explained by $\boldsymbol{\theta}_{A_j}$ and one not. That section illustrates how the corresponding analysis of variance provides insight into the alternative models and identifies ancillary statistics.

3.2.1 Features (or Checking Functions)

The choice of features in a prior predictive analysis is subjective and is driven by the application of the

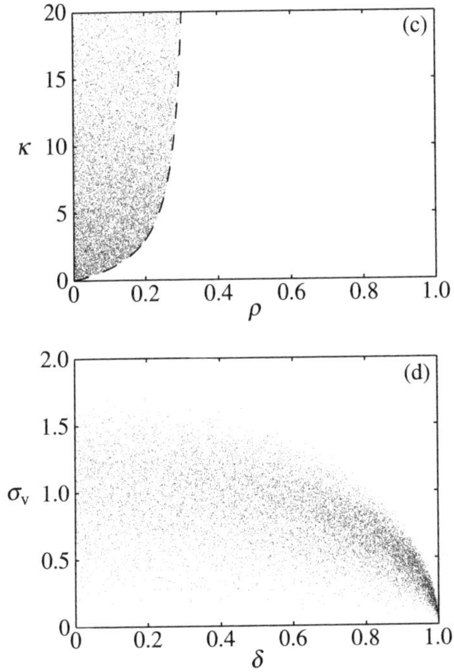

Figure 3.6. (*Continued.*) (c) Prior distribution of ρ and κ. (d) Prior distribution of δ and σ_v.

model at hand. In a specific decision-making application the vector of interest $\boldsymbol{\omega}_T$ might coincide with the arguments of the utility function $U(\boldsymbol{\omega}_T; \boldsymbol{d}_T)$. For example, in the illustrative problem here the utility function might be the return from a trading rule, and the functions of interest might then be the returns from several such rules. A model predicting returns from trading rules conflicting with those actually observed would be a cause for concern.

The illustration here is not linked to a specific decision and the features are chosen with reference to

Table 3.1. Features of the S&P 500 return series.

Feature	Data
Return mean × 100	0.810
Return standard deviation × 100	5.515
Months in bear markets	350
Largest bear market decline	0.846
Return skewness	−0.437
Return excess kurtosis	8.166
Ratio of range to standard deviation	12.451
Return autocorrelation, lag 1	0.078
Squared return autocorrelation, lag 1	0.242
Squared return autocorrelation, lag 12	0.182
Absolute return long-memory parameter	0.693

the statistical properties of the returns and the subsequent analyses in sections 3.2.3 and 3.3. There are eleven features and these are indicated in table 3.1 along with their corresponding observed values. The first four features of returns pertain to the drift in the price index: the mean and standard deviation of returns, the total number of months in bear markets, and the largest decline in a bear market. The next three features describe the shape and spread of the distribution of returns: the sample skewness and kurtosis coefficients, and the ratio of the range to the standard deviation.

The last four features are characteristics of the dynamics of returns. All have received at least some emphasis in the extensive literature on econometric modeling of equity returns. A conventional non-Bayesian analysis with a Gaussian model yields a statistically significant first-order autocorrelation coefficient. The positive sample first-order autocorrelation coefficient for squared returns is consistent with persistence in volatility. The sample twelfth-order autocorrelation coefficient for the squared return is also evidence of such persistence, but the relative values of the two statistics appear to be inconsistent with simple geometric decay in the autocorrelation function. The final feature is also evidence of long persistence in volatility and is widely interpreted as a stylized characteristic of asset returns. The data value shown is the GPH estimate $\hat{d}$ of the long-memory parameter using the lowest $T^{1/2} = 31$ harmonic periodogram ordinates (Geweke and Porter-Hudak 1984).

The observed features lead immediately to the non-Bayesian method of moments estimates $\hat{\rho} = 0.242$ and $\hat{\kappa} = 8.166$. Since $\hat{\kappa}/3(\hat{\kappa} + 2) = 0.268$, from (3.10) and (3.20) these point estimates are inconsistent with the GARCH model but consistent with the SV model. However, to equate population moments with sample moments, without consideration of the distribution of the sample moments, is always treacherous; section 4.4 demonstrates this in an entirely different context. It is especially unreliable here because the sampling standard deviation of $\hat{\kappa}$ depends on the eighth moment of the return y_t. Not only the size of this moment is in doubt in the context of the GARCH model, its very existence is.

3.2.2 Results

Figures 3.7, 3.8, and 3.10 show prior predictive densities for all but the first two features listed in table 3.1, computed from (3.21), (3.22) with $M = 10^4$. Each panel displays a histogram from the simulations as well as an approximate probability density function computed using a conventional Gaussian kernel with

Table 3.2. Inverse prior cumulative distribution functions of features.

Feature	Inverse c.d.f. at data		
	Gauss	GARCH	SV
Return mean	0.50	0.50	0.52
Return standard deviation	0.52	0.54	0.51
Months in bear markets	0.49	0.55	0.53
Largest bear market decline	0.91	0.90	0.91
Return skewness	0.00	0.03	0.16
Return excess kurtosis	1.00	0.98	0.74
Ratio of range to standard deviation	1.00	0.66	0.68
Return autocorrelation, lag 1	0.99	0.96	0.96
Squared return autocorrelation, lag 1	1.00	0.51	0.88
Squared return autocorrelation, lag 12	1.00	0.91	0.98
Absolute return long-memory parameter	1.00	0.97	0.99

standard deviation $25[\widehat{\text{var}}(z^{(m)})/M]^{1/2}$. In each panel the vertical line denotes the data point from table 3.1. The range of the horizontal axis is taken sufficiently wide to include all 10^4 simulated values of the feature, and widened further if necessary to include the data point. Consequently, the scaling for a given panel can vary across the three figures. Table 3.2 provides the values of all eleven prior predictive cumulative distribution functions evaluated at the observed values in table 3.1, $P(z_T \leqslant z_T^o \mid A_j)$, for the three models.

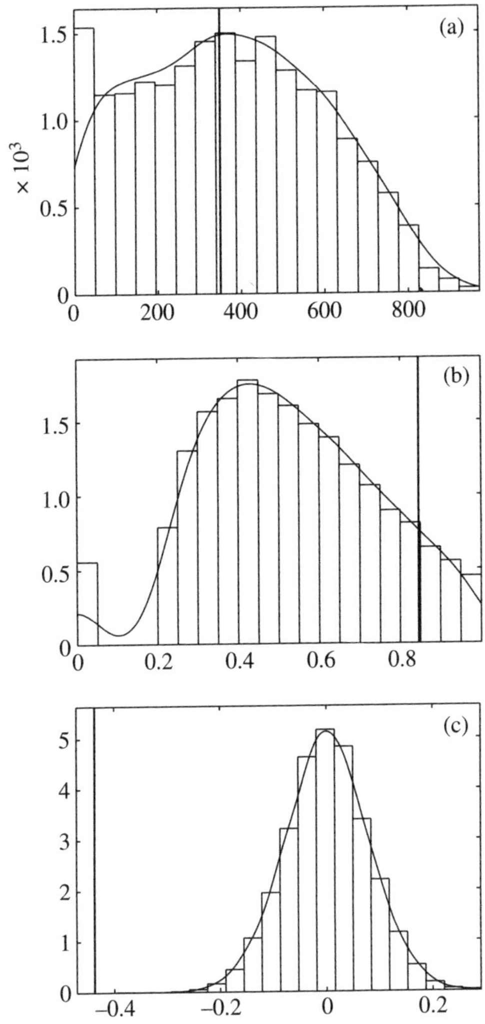

Figure 3.7. Prior predictive densities of some features in the Gaussian model (vertical lines indicate data values). (a) Months in bear markets. (b) Largest bear market decline. (c) Return skewness.

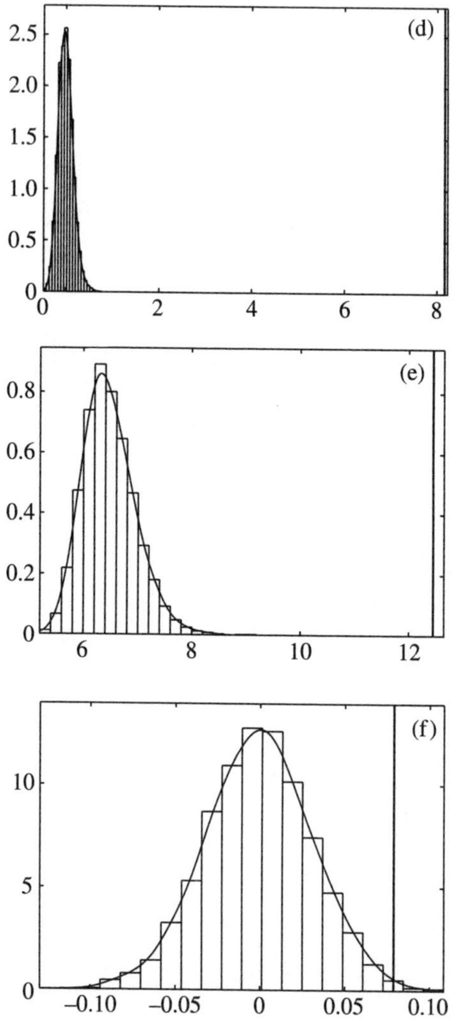

Figure 3.7. (*Continued.*) (d) Excess kurtosis of returns. (e) Ratio of range to standard deviation. (f) Return autocorrelation, lag 1.

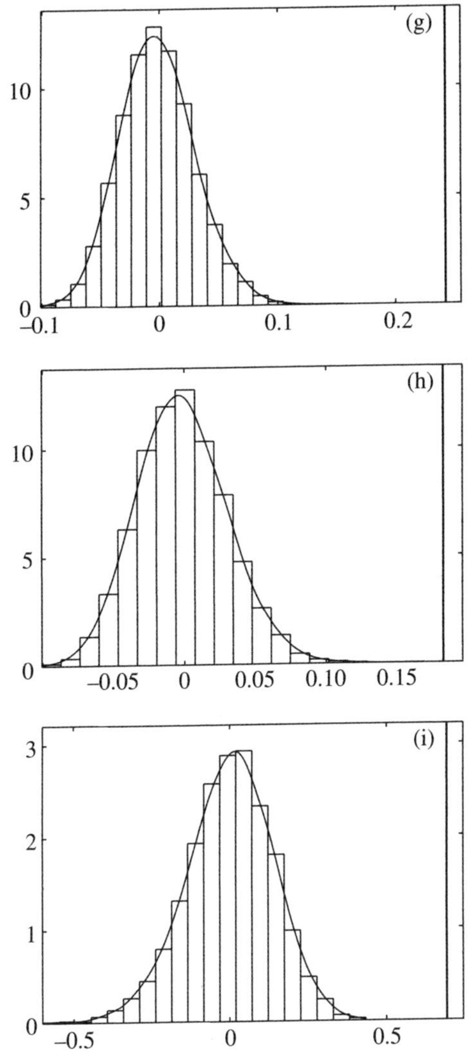

Figure 3.7. (*Continued.*) (g) Squared return autocorrelation, lag 1. (h) Squared return autocorrelation, lag 12. (i) Absolute return long-memory parameter.

Figure 3.7 and the corresponding column of table 3.2 convey the well-documented failure of the Gaussian model of asset returns. A sufficiently diffuse prior will always include the sample mean and the standard deviation of the return series. That is true here, by design of the prior: compare (3.1) and (3.2) with the values in the first two lines of table 3.1. It is not surprising that the prior seems to account for the bear market observations as well. The last seven features are all ancillary statistics in the Gaussian model, with $p(z_T \mid \boldsymbol{\theta}_A, A) = p(z_T \mid A)$ for all $\boldsymbol{\theta}_A \in \Theta_A$. Therefore the corresponding predictive densities in figure 3.7 would be the same for any prior density $p(\mu, \sigma^2 \mid A)$ in a Gaussian return model A.

Figure 3.8 provides prior predictive densities from the GARCH model for the same features. The densities for the bear market features are remarkably similar to those from the Gaussian model. This result is consistent with the occurrence and persistence of cycles being driven almost entirely by the first two moments of returns, whose prior distributions are the same in the two models. The predictive distribution of the return sample autocorrelation is a little more diffuse in the GARCH model than it is in the Gaussian model.

In contrast, the prior distributions of the other six features that are portrayed are dramatically different.[2] The prior predictive distributions of features associated with volatility dynamics, shown in panels (g)–(i) of the figures, are all much more diffuse than in the Gaussian model. They are also clearly much more in line with the data. This is evident in (1) the values of $p(z_T^o \mid A)$, which are orders of magnitude larger in

[2] Note the very different scaling of the horizontal axis for some of the same panels in figures 3.7 and 3.8.

the GARCH model than in the Gaussian model, and in (2) the values of α_{pre}, suggested by Box (1980) and presented in table 3.2, that are more favorable to the GARCH model than they are to the Gaussian model.

The prior predictive distributions of the sample skewness and kurtosis coefficients, in panels (c) and (d) of figure 3.8, are remarkable. The range of the horizontal axis, which is taken just wide enough to include all 10^4 simulations, is driven by the fact that population sixth moments (in the case of skewness) and population eighth moments (in the case of kurtosis) fail to exist for virtually all of the (α_1, β_1) values supported by the prior distribution, as indicated in figure 3.5. This is evident from comparing panel (g) of this figure with the ranges for existence of higher moments indicated in figure 1 of Bollerslev (1986). That is why, despite the fact that the prior distribution for the coefficient of population kurtosis supports very high values, the observed value is in the ninety-eighth percentile of the prior predictive distribution of the sample kurtosis coefficient for $T = 984$. The GARCH model does not account well for the leptokurtosis and the skewness of observed returns simultaneously.

This limitation becomes even more evident in bivariate prior predictive distributions. The leading example is the joint distribution of the sample first-order autocorrelation coefficient of squared returns and the sample excess kurtosis coefficient. Figure 3.9 provides the log prior predictive joint density of these two features, constructed using the multivariate Gaussian copula described in section 3.4. The contours show the difference between the log predictive density at its maximum and the points in the figure. The distribution is somewhat similar to the prior distribution of the corresponding population moments shown in figure 3.5,

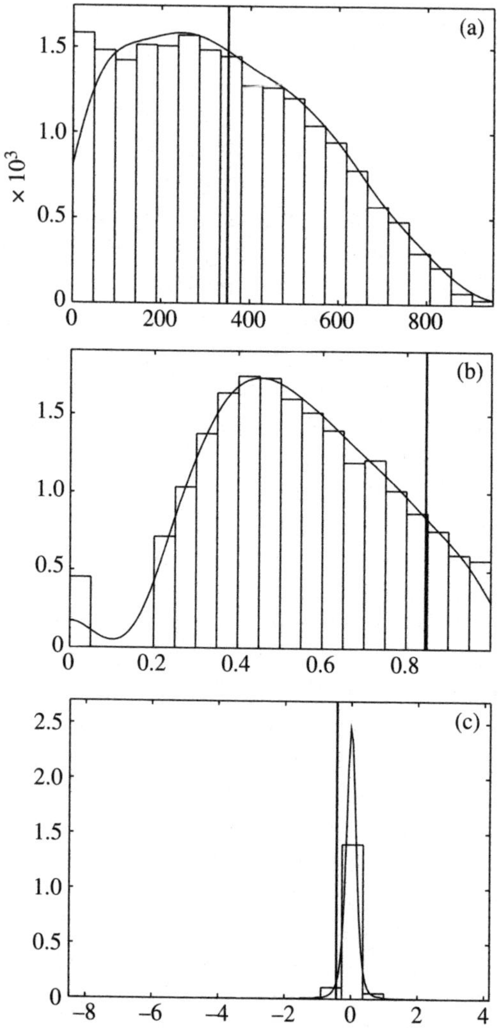

Figure 3.8. Prior predictive densities of some features in the GARCH(1, 1) model (vertical lines indicate data values). (a) Months in bear markets. (b) Largest bear market decline. (c) Return skewness.

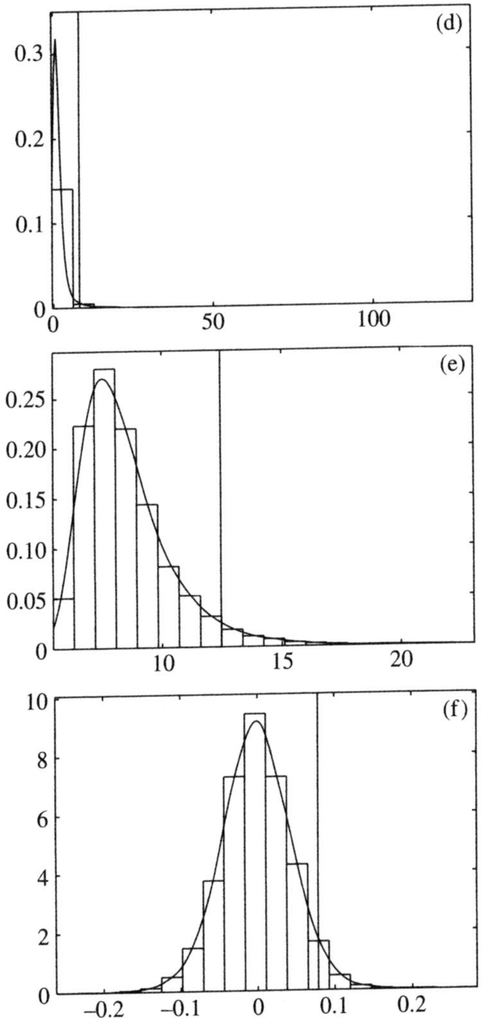

Figure 3.8. (*Continued.*) (d) Excess kurtosis of returns. (e) Ratio of range to standard deviation. (f) Return autocorrelation, lag 1.

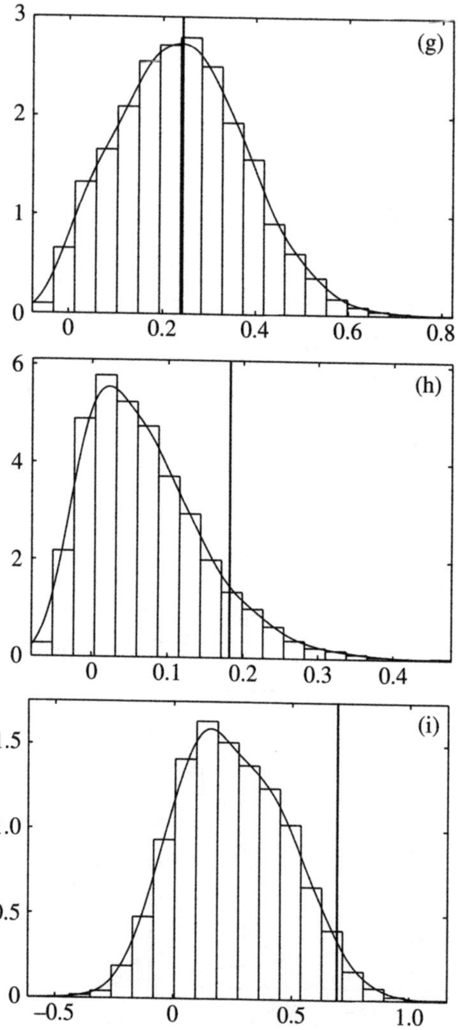

Figure 3.8. (*Continued.*) (g) Squared return autocorrelation, lag 1. (h) Squared return autocorrelation, lag 12. (i) Absolute return long-memory parameter.

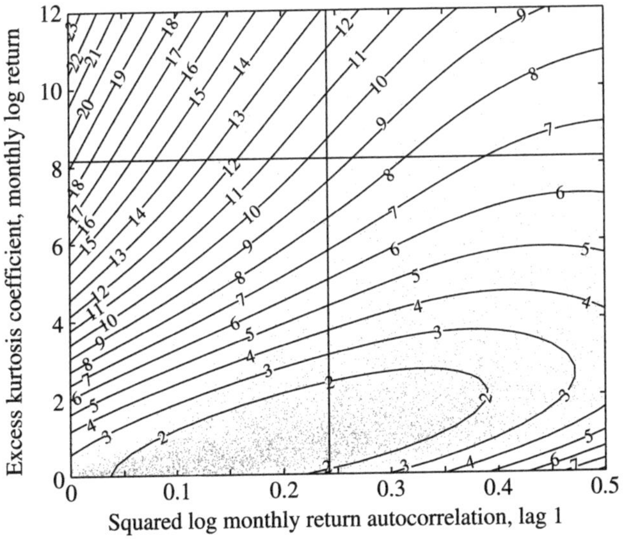

Figure 3.9. The contours show the level of the log prior predictive density below the maximum. The dots show 4,000 draws from the prior predictive distribution. The intersection of the horizontal and vertical lines indicates the data point.

but it concentrates more on low values of excess kurtosis. In general, prior predictive distributions of sample moments converge to prior predictive distributions of the corresponding population moments, but convergence is slower the higher the moments, and especially slow when a central limit theorem does not govern convergence due to the failure of the requisite higher-order moments to exist. That is the case here. (Geweke (1986) elaborates on this point in the context of the GARCH model.)

Figure 3.10 shows the univariate prior predictive distributions of the same nine features in the SV model. This model is a vast improvement on the Gaussian

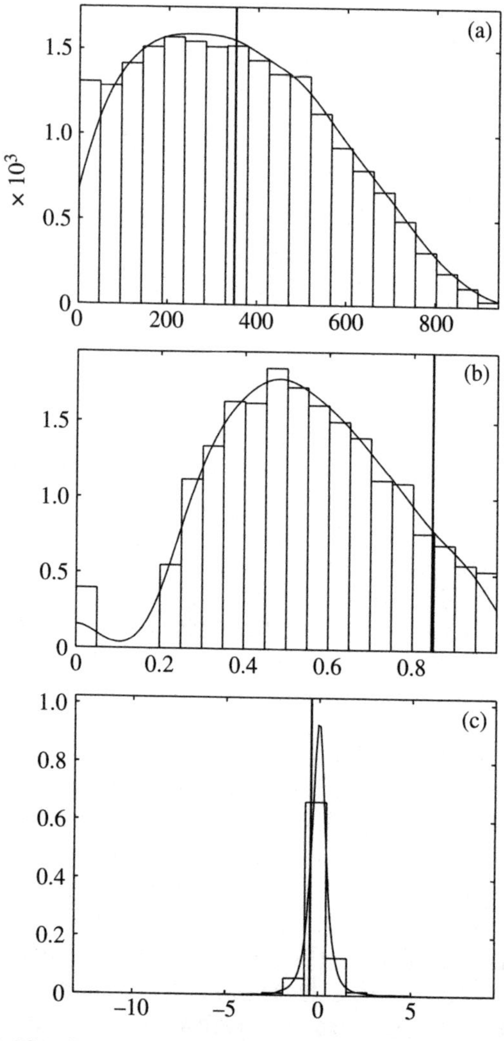

Figure 3.10. Prior predictive densities of features in the SV model (vertical lines indicate data values). (a) Months in bear markets. (b) Largest bear market decline. (c) Return skewness.

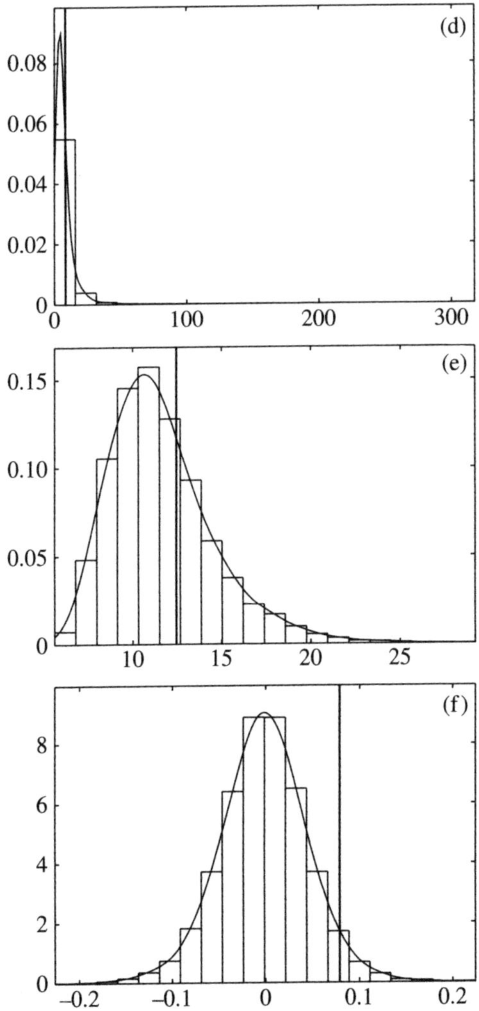

Figure 3.10. (*Continued.*) (d) Excess kurtosis of returns. (e) Ratio of range to standard deviation. (f) Return autocorrelation, lag 1.

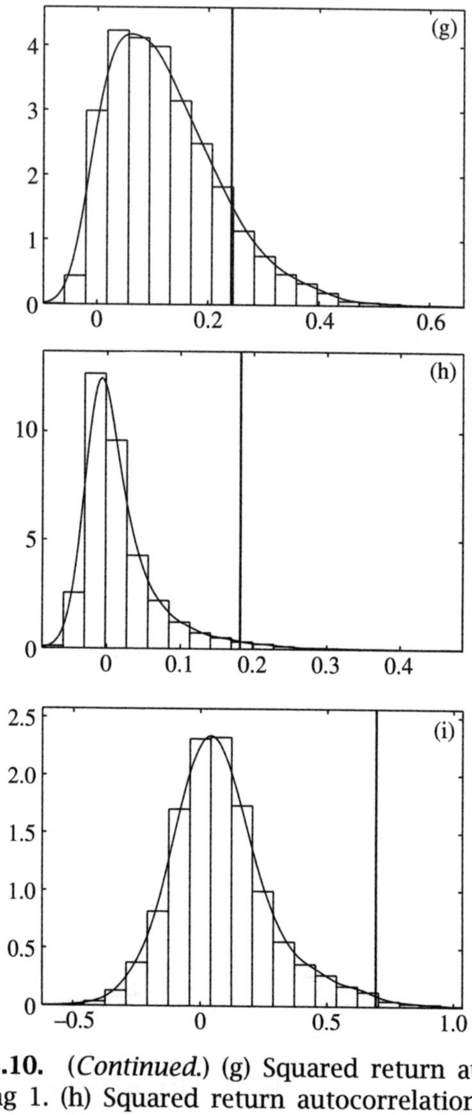

Figure 3.10. (*Continued.*) (g) Squared return autocorrelation, lag 1. (h) Squared return autocorrelation, lag 12. (i) Absolute return long-memory parameter.

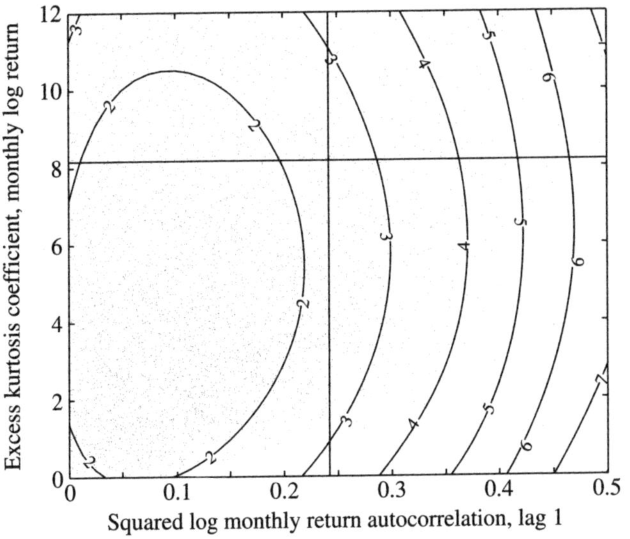

Figure 3.11. The contours show the level of the log predictive density below the maximum for the GARCH model. The dots show 4,000 draws from the prior predictive distribution. The intersection of the horizontal and vertical lines indicates the data point.

model in the same way that the GARCH model is. Comparison of figures 3.10 and 3.8 shows that the SV model has greater consistency with the observed dispersion of returns, but the GARCH model is more consistent with volatility dynamics.

This comparison becomes especially evident in the prior predictive joint distribution of these two moments. Figure 3.11 provides the same joint log prior predictive density for the SV model that figure 3.9 does for the GARCH model, for the same range of sample moments. The scale of the log predictive density is also the same: the contours in figure 3.11 are measured relative to the peak of the GARCH log predictive density in figure 3.9. The log predictive density in the SV model, evaluated at the observed values, is about -2.5. This is substantially greater than the log predictive density in the GARCH model, which is about -8.5. Highest predictive density regions of conventional size for these moments are more concentrated in the GARCH model than in the SV model. Notice that the data point is excluded from such regions in the former model but included in the latter one. Section 3.3 pursues this analysis in higher dimensions.

3.2.3 Prior Predictive Analysis of Variance

For any feature z_T for which $\mathrm{E}(z_T^2 \mid A) < \infty$, the Rao–Blackwell theorem implies that

$$\mathrm{var}(z_T \mid A) = \mathrm{var}_{\boldsymbol{\theta}_A}[\mathrm{E}(z_T \mid \boldsymbol{\theta}_A, A)] + \mathrm{E}_{\boldsymbol{\theta}_A}[\mathrm{var}(z_T \mid \boldsymbol{\theta}_A, A)]. \tag{3.23}$$

Loosely speaking, (3.23) attributes uncertainty about z_T to two sources: uncertainty about $\boldsymbol{\theta}_A$ and intrinsic uncertainty about z_T that would exist even if $\boldsymbol{\theta}_A$ were known. This section focuses on

$$f(z_T \mid A) = \frac{\mathrm{var}_{\boldsymbol{\theta}_A}[\mathrm{E}(z_T \mid \boldsymbol{\theta}_A, A)]}{\mathrm{var}(z_T \mid A)},$$

which is the fraction of the prior predictive variance in z_T due to the prior variance in $\boldsymbol{\theta}_A$.

The decomposition can be approximated with arbitrary accuracy using a minor extension of the prior predictive simulator described earlier in this chapter. For each of the simulated parameter values $\boldsymbol{\theta}_A^{(m)} \sim p(\boldsymbol{\theta}_A \mid A)$, simulate

$$z_T^{(m,r)} \sim p(z_T \mid \boldsymbol{\theta}_A^{(m)}) \quad (r = 1, \dots, R),$$

and define

$$\bar{z}_T^{(m)} = R^{-1} \sum_{r=1}^{R} z_T^{(m,r)} \quad (r = 1, \dots, R)$$

and

$$\bar{\bar{z}}_T = M^{-1} \sum_{m=1}^{M} \bar{z}_T^{(m)}.$$

(The extension of the simulator consists of the additional $R-1$ simulations of z_T corresponding to each $\boldsymbol{\theta}_A^{(m)}$.) A classical one-way analysis of variance with balanced design then provides a simulation-consistent estimate of the decomposition (3.23). As $M, R \to \infty$,

$$(MR)^{-1} \sum_{m=1}^{M} \sum_{r=1}^{R} (z_T^{(m,r)} - \bar{\bar{z}}_T)^2 \xrightarrow{\text{a.s.}} \text{var}(z_T \mid A),$$

$$M^{-1} \sum_{m=1}^{M} (\bar{z}_T^{(m)} - \bar{\bar{z}}_T)^2 \xrightarrow{\text{a.s.}} \text{var}_{\boldsymbol{\theta}_A}[\text{E}(z_T \mid \boldsymbol{\theta}_A, A)],$$

$$\hat{f}(z_T \mid A) = \frac{R \sum_{m=1}^{M} (\bar{z}_T^{(m)} - \bar{\bar{z}}_T)^2}{\sum_{m=1}^{M} \sum_{r=1}^{R} (z_T^{(m,r)} - \bar{\bar{z}}_T)^2} \xrightarrow{\text{a.s.}} f(z_T \mid A).$$

Suppose that the prior distribution is substantively diffuse: that is, that it provides substantial support for all reasonable, and perhaps some unreasonable, values of $\boldsymbol{\theta}_A$. Suppose also that $f(z_T \mid A) \approxeq 0$. Then, if the prior predictive distribution indicates that z_T^o is implausible, the difficulty lies with the specification of $p(\boldsymbol{y}_T \mid \boldsymbol{\theta}_A)$ and not with $p(\boldsymbol{\theta}_A \mid A)$. The limiting case $f(z_T \mid A) = 0$ is instructive.

Proposition 3.1. *If z_T is an ancillary statistic in the model A, then $f(z_T \mid A) = 0$.*

Proof. By definition (Casella and Berger 2002, p. 282), $p(z_T \mid \boldsymbol{\theta}_A, A) = p(z_T \mid A)$. Then $\mathrm{E}(z_T \mid \boldsymbol{\theta}_A, A) = \mathrm{E}(z_T \mid A)$ and so $f(z_T \mid A) = 0$. □

The converse of this result is false, the simplest counterexample perhaps being

$$P(\theta = 1, z = 0) = \tfrac{1}{2},$$
$$P(\theta = 0, z = -1) = P(\theta = 0, z = 1) = \tfrac{1}{4}.$$

If $f(z_T \mid A) = 0$, then

$$\frac{M(R-1)}{M-1} \cdot \frac{\hat{f}(z_T \mid A)}{1 - \hat{f}(z_T \mid A)} \mathrel{\dot{\sim}} F(M-1, M(R-1)),$$

leading to a consistent test of the hypothesis $f(z_T \mid A) = 0$. Thus it is possible to show that z_T is not ancillary using the analysis of variance proposed here. The conclusion $f(z_T \mid A) = 0$ does not imply that z_T is ancillary, but finding $f(g(z_T) \mid A) = 0$ for a number of alternative nonlinear transformations g would strongly suggest that z_T is, indeed, an ancillary statistic. As a by-product the prior predictive simulations supporting that conjecture would then provide rejection regions for conventional non-Bayesian specification tests.

In principle it is possible to establish analytically whether z_T is ancillary, but in practice this is far from clear and the analytical exercise may be impracticably difficult. Moreover, while the ancillarity of z_T is critical to a non-Bayesian specification test, the focus here is more qualitative: whether or not changes in the prior distribution would lead to substantially different conclusions about $p(z_T^o \mid A)$.

Table 3.3 provides analysis of variance in the prior predictive distribution of the features introduced in section 3.2.1, for the three models and the data set discussed in section 3.1. As indicated in the table, three of the features were transformed to assure finite variance in the prior predictive distributions in all three models.

For the i.i.d. Gaussian model, the prior predictive analysis of variance reflects the well-known fact that location- and scale-invariant statistics are ancillary. In the GARCH and SV models no feature in table 3.3 is an ancillary statistic. In the case of skewness and the return autocorrelation at lag 1 this is evident only after an appropriate transformation of the feature, because in these two cases means are zero conditional on any values of the model parameters. For most of the features, substantial portions of prior predictive variance are due both to variation in parameters and to variance conditional on parameters.

With the exception of return autocorrelation at lag 1, substantial fractions of the prior predictive variances of the features studied are due to prior variation in the model parameters. The important implication for prior predictive analysis is that model checking based on these features is sensitive to the prior distribution of parameters as well as to the distribution of observables conditional on parameters. In the absence of strong substantive information about the parameters, it is important to avoid dogmatic or near-dogmatic prior distributions. Doing so requires some substantive understanding of the model. As illustrated in parts (a) and (b) of figures 3.5 and 3.6, this can happen inadvertently if one resorts to seemingly vague or flat prior distributions in the parameter space.

Table 3.3. Analysis of variance, features of the S&P 500 return series.

	$[\mathrm{var}(z_T \mid A)]^{1/2}$ and $f(z_T \mid A)$					
Feature z_T	Gaussian		GARCH		SV	
Return mean $\times$ 100	0.359	**0.69**	0.366	**0.60**	0.347	**0.61**
Return standard deviation	0.026	**1.00**	0.031	**0.82**	0.032	**0.97**
Months in bear markets	215.4	**0.75**	214.4	**0.61**	209.1	**0.70**
Largest bear market decline	0.208	**0.77**	0.205	**0.58**	0.207	**0.70**
Return skewness[a]	0.069	0.01	0.152	0.01	0.284	0.01
|Return skewness[a]|	0.040	0.01	0.100	**0.11**	0.171	**0.25**
Return excess kurtosis[a]	0.013	0.01	0.244	**0.45**	0.170	**0.81**
Range/standard deviation[a]	0.008	0.01	0.018	**0.34**	0.018	**0.60**
Return AC, lag 1	0.031	0.01	0.046	0.01	0.044	0.01
|Return AC, lag 1|	0.019	0.01	0.029	**0.04**	0.028	**0.08**
Squared return AC lag 1	0.031	0.01	0.132	**0.59**	0.097	**0.57**
Squared return AC lag 12	0.031	0.01	0.078	**0.40**	0.054	**0.54**
Absolute return long memory $\hat{d}$	0.137	*0.01*	0.233	**0.55**	0.205	**0.55**

Bold numbers indicate a significantly positive level at 0.001; italic numbers indicate a significantly positive level at 0.05. Results are based on 10,000 simulations with $M = R = 100$.

[a]Transformation $z_T/(1 + |z_T|)$ has been applied.

3.3 Comparison with an Incomplete Model

A significant limitation of Bayesian model comparison described in section 2.4 is the conditioning on a particular set of well-articulated models. It may well be the case that none of these models account well for "stylized facts" or other aspects of the data that are thought to be important for the purposes at hand. Bayesian methods in particular place probability distributions on all knowable quantities, and these distributions imply restrictions on what may happen, or could have happened. If events transpire that are improbable under all of the well-articulated models, then one has little confidence in the set of models being used. This set of circumstances can be revealed by non-Bayesian methods, for example in frequentist testing of restrictions against unspecified alternatives. A Bayesian model in which these deficiencies do not emerge is said to be well-calibrated (Dawid 1984; Little 2006). Prior predictive analyses, described in sections 2.4.1 and 3.2, and posterior predictive analyses, discussed in section 2.4.2, are designed to uncover the same problems. As argued in section 2.4.2, the former are Bayesian and the latter are not.

One conclusion might be that inference under a specified set of models should be Bayesian but that assessment of these models can and should involve non-Bayesian ideas. (For an alternative conclusion see Poirier (1988), especially pp. 138–41.) In particular, such a synthesis of Bayesian and frequentist ideas has been advocated by many, including prominent Bayesians like Berger (2000). This is an interesting challenge to the conjecture that economists and other scientists act like Bayesians, rather than frequentists. There is no doubt that these investigators look for deficiencies in well-specified models using frequentist methods, using hypothesis tests and p-values as well as less formal steps. But judicious application of frequentist methods can also amount to Bayesian learning using available technology—an idea familiar to econometricians from Leamer (1978).

Prior predictive analyses, described in sections 2.4.1 and 3.2, and posterior predictive analyses, discussed in section 2.4.2, can be used to assess models. They can lead one to conclude that a model is deficient, or preforms poorly, for a particular purpose. But such analyses, whether Bayesian or not, raise the question: deficient or poor performance compared with what? If one is to reject all models under consideration as deficient, then there must be at least a tacit belief that there exist models that perform better, together with some notion of how well these models perform. This section puts these ideas in a formal Bayesian context.

3.3.1 Methods

If one were certain that a set of complete models $A_1, \ldots, A_n$ included all possible models for $\mathbf{y}$, no model-validation exercise could have a disconcerting outcome. Indeed, there would then be no reason to engage in model validation, but the fact that these exercises are a critical part of good econometric work reflects the fact that one (or, at any rate, one's audience) is never so certain. More importantly, one often has incompletely articulated ideas about reasonable distributions for checking functions z_i $(i = 1, \ldots, q)$. An informal model of some kind for the z_i seems essential to the choice of checking functions, driven by the characteristics that the investigator thinks a good model ought to have. To formalize this notion, associate a model B_i with each checking function z_i, of the form $p(z_i \mid B_i)$. A natural extension of this idea is an incomplete model $p(z_1, \ldots, z_q \mid B)$ for the q checking functions. These models may be incomplete, in the sense that they cannot be (or at least have not been) derived as prior predictive distributions from any complete model for $\boldsymbol{y}$. Therefore, the models B_i may not even be known to be coherent: that is, it may not be known whether there exists a model A such that $p(\boldsymbol{\theta}_A \mid A)$ and $p(\boldsymbol{y} \mid \boldsymbol{\theta}_A, A)$ yield $p(z_i \mid A) = p(z_i \mid B_i)$ $(i = 1, \ldots, q)$, or $p(z_1, \ldots, z_q \mid B)$ if a joint incomplete model is being entertained.

The incomplete models B_i allow one to compare the complete models in hand (the A_i) with as-yet incompletely specified alternatives, using formally justified Bayesian methods. The purpose of this exercise is to model what econometricians do implicitly in their day-to-day work, and to elucidate the corresponding formal procedures. To see how this idea works, suppose that for a group of features $\boldsymbol{z}_T^o$, approximations to $p(\boldsymbol{z}_T^o \mid A_i)$ $(i = 1, \ldots, n)$ are available. (These approximations will typically be constructed from simulations $\boldsymbol{z}_T^{(m)} \sim p(\boldsymbol{z}_T \mid A_i)$ $(m = 1, \ldots, M)$ using nonparametric or semiparametric methods. Section 3.3.2 provides more detail, but these considerations limit the length of $\boldsymbol{z}_T$.) Typically, the incomplete model B consists of independent distributions for each of the q components of $\boldsymbol{z}_T$, with the distribution $z_{Ti} \mid B_i$ chosen so that $p(z_{Ti}^o \mid B_i)$ can be evaluated directly and then

$$p(\boldsymbol{z}_T^o \mid B) = \prod_{i=1}^{q} p(z_{Ti}^o \mid B_i).$$

It is now possible to assess the evidence in the observed $\boldsymbol{z}_T^o$ about the complete models $A_1, \ldots, A_n$ and the incomplete model B. Indeed, this is the only basis of comparison with B because that model speaks only to $\boldsymbol{z}_T$, not to $\boldsymbol{y}_T$. In particular, the Bayes factor in favor of model A_i versus the incomplete model B is $p(\boldsymbol{z}_T^o \mid A_i)/p(\boldsymbol{z}_T^o \mid B)$. If it is not possible to assess $p(\boldsymbol{z}_T^o \mid A_i)$ with sufficient accuracy, then it may be possible to undertake the exercise with subsets of $\boldsymbol{z}_T^o$; indeed, this may be instructive in any event because it may lead to a conclusion that a model A_i is adequate in some respects but not in others.

This exercise can be carried out even when there is only one complete model under consideration. Bayes factors in favor of models will of course be sensitive to the specific choice of incomplete model, and different investigators will use different incomplete models B. These differences are unavoidable, and even desirable: especially in the model formulation stage, different economists have different ideas about what a model ought to be able to achieve. Moreover, investigators are likely to change formal prior densities $p(\boldsymbol{\theta}_A \mid A)$ as they observe the implications for $p(\boldsymbol{z}_T \mid A)$. This is also desirable if features $\boldsymbol{z}_T$ have been chosen at least in part because they help interpret the implications of models. In general, the minimal standard $p(\boldsymbol{z}_T^o \mid A)/p(\boldsymbol{z}_T^o \mid B) > 1$ would appear reasonable for the complete model A.

To the extent that the elements of $\boldsymbol{z}_T$ capture the same qualitative aspects of the model, one might expect $p(\boldsymbol{z}_T^o \mid A)/p(\boldsymbol{z}_T^o \mid B)$ to be even larger, because A enforces coherence while B does not. As a simple example, suppose that the sample mean z_{T1} and sample median z_{T2} of $\boldsymbol{y}_T$ constitute the two features in $\boldsymbol{z}_T$ capturing central tendency, and the incomplete model specifies independent distributions for the two features each embracing all reasonable values for central tendency. In the plausible case in which A enforces strong correlation between the mean z_{T1} and the median z_{T2}, and in the event that A provides support for the indicators of central tendency reflected in $z^o_{T1} \approx z^o_{T2}$, $p(\mathbf{z}^o_T \mid A)/p(\mathbf{z}^o_T \mid B) \gg 1$ because $p(\mathbf{z}_T \mid A)$ concentrates its support on $z_{T1} \approx z_{T2}$.

3.3.2 Application

The prior distributions detailed in table 3.4 provide components of an incomplete model B for $\mathbf{z}_T$. For each of the eleven features i described in section 3.2, the prior distributions listed in table 3.4 provide the functional form and the parameters of the densities $p(z_{Ti} \mid B_i)$.

The nine panels of figure 3.12 display all but the first two prior densities $p(z_{Ti} \mid B_i)$ of the incomplete model as solid curves. The panels also incorporate the prior predictive densities from each of the three models that were displayed separately in figures 3.7, 3.8, and 3.10. The solid vertical line indicates the observed value of the feature from table 3.1 in each case. In the panel corresponding to feature i the value of $p(z^o_{Ti} \mid B)$ is indicated by the intersection of the solid vertical line with the solid curve; the value of $p(z^o_{Ti} \mid A_1)$ for the Gaussian model A_1 is indicated by the intersection with the dotted curve; the value of $p(z^o_{Ti} \mid A_2)$ for the GARCH model A_2 is indicated by the intersection with the dash-dotted curve; and the value of $p(z^o_{Ti} \mid A_3)$ for the SV model A_3 is indicated by the intersection with the dashed curve.

Feature by feature, each model A_i can be evaluated by comparison with the incomplete model B using figure 3.12. In the case of the price drift features (months in bear markets and largest bear market decline),

$$p(z^o_{Ti} \mid A_j)/p(z^o_{Ti} \mid B) > 1$$

Table 3.4. Prior distributions of features in the incomplete model.

Feature	Incomplete model prior distribution: Functional form	Mean	St. dev.
Return mean × 100	Gaussian	0.8	0.3
Return standard deviation × 100	$\sigma^{-2} \sim$ Gamma	0.62	0.31
Months in bear markets	Uniform$(0, T)$	$T/2$	$12^{-1/2}\mathrm{T}$
Largest bear market decline	$\propto (1-f)^2 I_{(0.2,1)}(f)$	0.4	0.155
Return skewness	Gaussian	0	1
Return excess kurtosis	Exponential	8	8
Ratio of range to standard deviation	1 + Gamma	7	3
Return autocorrelation, lag 1	Gaussian	0	0.1
Squared return autocorrelation, lag 1	Uniform$(0, 1)$	1/5	$12^{1/2}$
Squared return autocorrelation, lag 12	Beta	0.25	0.25
Absolute return long-memory parameter	Gaussian	0.5	0.25

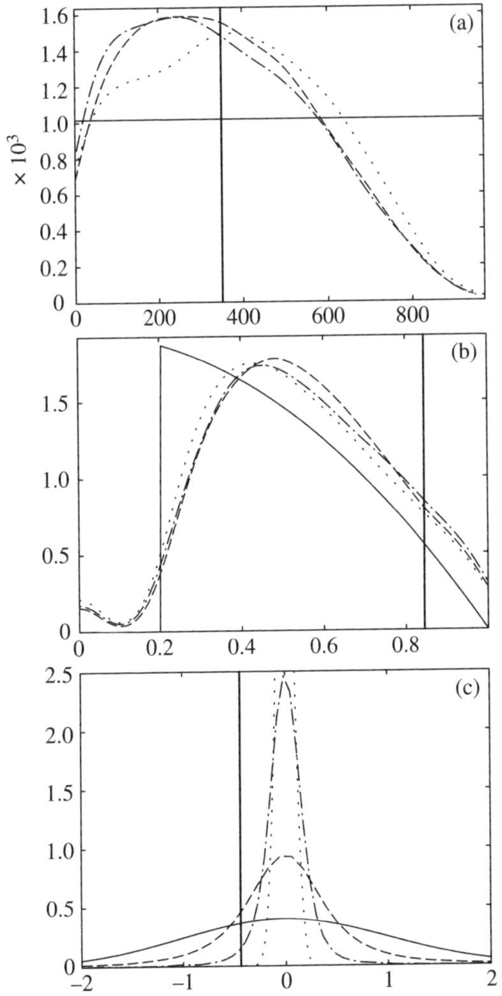

Figure 3.12. The prior predictive densities of features in the Gaussian (dotted), GARCH (dash-dotted), SV (dashed), and incomplete (solid) models. The solid vertical line indicates the observed value. (a) Months in bear markets. (b) Largest bear market decline. (c) Return skewness.

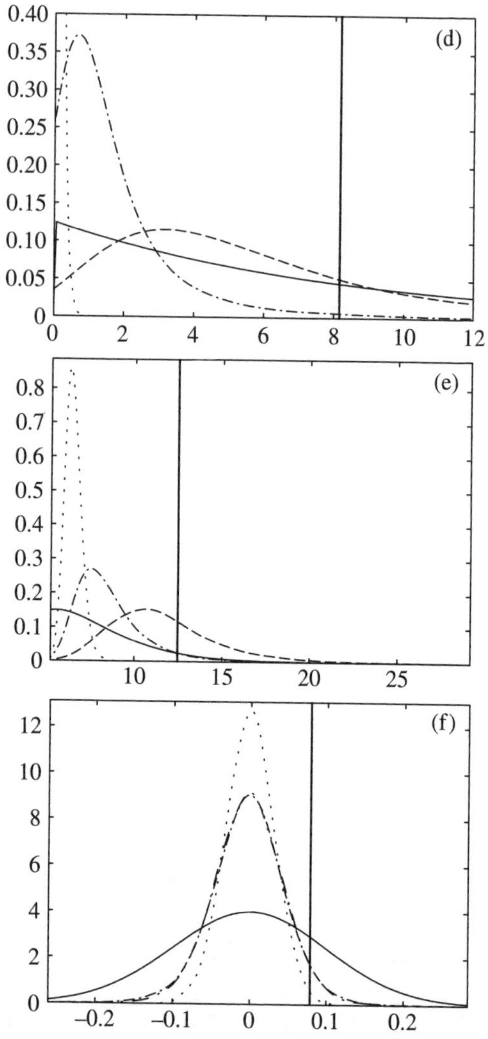

Figure 3.12. (*Continued.*) (d) Excess kurtosis of returns. (e) Ratio of range to standard deviation. (f) Return autocorrelation, lag 1.

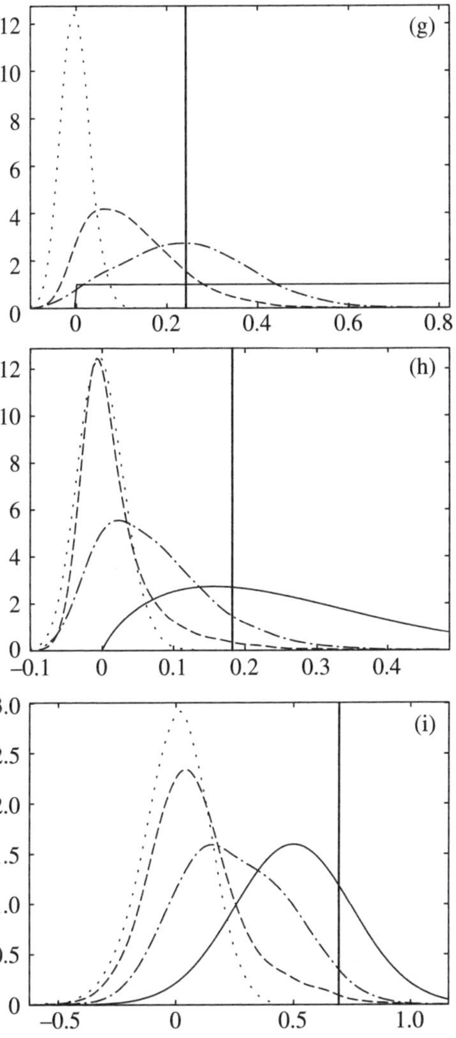

Figure 3.12. (*Continued.*) (g) Squared return autocorrelation, lag 1. (h) Squared return autocorrelation, lag 12. (i) Absolute return long-memory parameter.

for all three complete models. For return skewness,

$$p(z_{Ti}^o \mid A_j)/p(z_{Ti}^o \mid B) \approxeq 1$$

in the case of the GARCH and SV models, but the Gaussian model does not compare well with the incomplete model. In the case of kurtosis,

$$p(z_{Ti}^o \mid A_j)/p(z_{Ti}^o \mid B) \approxeq 1$$

only for the SV model;

$$p(z_{Ti}^o \mid A_j)/p(z_{Ti}^o \mid B) < 1$$

for the GARCH model and

$$p(z_{Ti}^o \mid A_j)/p(z_{Ti}^o \mid B) \ll 1$$

for the Gaussian model. For the alternative measure of dispersion, ratio of range to standard deviation,

$$p(z_{Ti}^o \mid A_j)/p(z_{Ti}^o \mid B) > 1$$

for the SV model,

$$p(z_{Ti}^o \mid A_j)/p(z_{Ti}^o \mid B) \approxeq 1$$

for the GARCH model, and

$$p(z_{Ti}^o \mid A_j)/p(z_{Ti}^o \mid B) \ll 1$$

in the case of the Gaussian model. For the sample first-order autocorrelation coefficient, $p(z_{Ti}^o \mid A_j)$ falls short of $p(z_{Ti}^o \mid B)$ in all three models, but much more so for the i.i.d. Gaussian model. For the sample first-order autocorrelation coefficient of squared returns in both the SV and GARCH models,

$$p(z_{Ti}^o \mid A_j)/p(z_{Ti}^o \mid B) > 1,$$

Table 3.5. Log Bayes factors in favor of each model over the incomplete model, for four groups of features.

	Gaussian	GARCH	SV
Price drift	−2.23	1.48	0.83
(four features)	−2.27	1.28	1.10
Return moments	−∞	−2.65	3.52
(three features)	−∞	−2.14	3.48
Return dynamics	−∞	−0.04	2.46
(four features)	−∞	−0.29	2.81
All eleven features	−∞	1.25	4.44
	−∞	1.15	3.82

whereas this Bayes factor is very small in the Gaussian model. On the other hand, for the sample twelfth-order autocorrelation coefficient of squared returns in all three models,

$$p(z^o_{Ti} \mid A_j)/p(z^o_{Ti} \mid B) < 1,$$

and the Gaussian model again does not fare well. Results are similar for the long-memory parameter for absolute returns, which is the alternative measure of long-run persistence in return volatility.

The interpretation of these results becomes clearer by examining Bayes factors for groups of features. Table 3.5 provides the log Bayes factor

$$\log[p(\boldsymbol{z}^o_T \mid A_j)/p(\boldsymbol{z}^o_T \mid B)]$$

for several configurations of a vector of features $\boldsymbol{z}_T$ and each of the three models A_j. In each case the densities were approximated using the Gaussian copula described in section 3.4, with smoothing parameter $c_i = 25[\text{var}(z^{(m)}_{Ti})/M]^{1/2}$, where M is the number of draws from the prior predictive distribution and $\text{var}(z_{Ti}^{(m)})$ is the sample variance of these M draws. (This is the same Gaussian copula smoothing parameter used to compute the contours of the predictive densities in figures 3.9 and 3.11.) For all entries $M = 5,000$. The computations were undertaken twice, with independent draws from the prior predictive distribution; the differences within the pairs of results provides a rough idea of the accuracy of the approximations of the densities.

The group of features labeled "price drift" is composed of the first four features in table 3.4: the sample mean and sample standard deviation of returns, the number of months in bear markets, and the largest bear market decline. For this group the Bayes factor favors the incomplete model by a ratio of about 10:1 over the Gaussian model. It mildly favors the GARCH and SV models over the incomplete model.

The group of features labeled "return moments" has three components: the sample skewness and excess kurtosis coefficients and the ratio of the range to the standard deviation. The sample of this group $\boldsymbol{z}_{Ti}^{(m)}$ drawn from the Gaussian prior predictive distribution is so far removed from $\boldsymbol{z}_T^o$ that approximation of $p(\boldsymbol{z}_T^o \mid A_j)$ is impossible; hence the entries $-\infty$ for the log Bayes factor. The GARCH model fails, with Bayes factors favoring the incomplete model by a ratio of about 10:1. On the other hand, the SV model receives strong support, with Bayes factors more than 30:1 in its favor.

The group of features labeled "return dynamics" consists of the last four features in table 3.4: the sample first-order autocorrelation coefficient of returns, the sample squared return autocorrelation coefficient at lags 1 and 12, and the long-memory parameter estimate for absolute returns. The Gaussian model, again, cannot come close to reproducing the observed vector of features. For the GARCH model,

$$p(\mathbf{z}_T^o \mid A_j)/p(\mathbf{z}_T^o \mid B) \approxeq 1,$$

while the Bayes factor favors the SV model over the incomplete model by a ratio of more than 10:1.

For all features combined, the Gaussian copula produces approximations of sufficient quality to assess both the absolute and relative performance of each of the three models. The Gaussian model fails. The Bayes factor weakly favors the GARCH model over the incomplete model, by a ratio of about 3:1. It strongly favors the SV model, the ratio being above 40:1. The results for the three subvectors are useful in the interpretation of this outcome. They show that the satisfactory evaluation of the GARCH model, overall, is compromised by its failure to account for observed higher sample moments of returns as well as the benchmark incomplete model does, and by doing no better than the incomplete model for return dynamics. This evaluation is especially telling given that the GARCH model is designed to account for these features. The results for the three subvectors also show that the strong performance of the SV model, in comparison with the incomplete model, is due to its ability to outperform the incomplete model in explaining higher-order sample moments and persistence in volatility.

Of course, all of these results depend on the specification of the incomplete model. Given the results in table 3.5, it is a matter of simple arithmetic to recompute Bayes factors against alternative specifications of the incomplete model so long as $p(\boldsymbol{z}_T^o \mid B)$ can be computed in closed form. While formulation of the incomplete model, like all models, is subjective, modifications of the incomplete model that still provide scope for a wide range of plausible observable features tend not to change the outcomes in table 3.5 very substantially. This can be appreciated best, perhaps, in the context of figure 3.12. The qualitative conclusion that the GARCH model is rejected against an incompletely specified alternative, while the SV model is accepted, is likely to stand under reformulations of the incomplete model.

3.4 Appendix: A Gaussian Copula for Evaluating Predictive Densities of Vector Functions of Interest

The random vector $\boldsymbol{z}$ has q components,

$$\boldsymbol{z}' = (z_1, \dots, z_q)'.$$

The problem is to approximate a p.d.f. $p(\boldsymbol{z})$ at a specified point $\boldsymbol{z}^o$, using M i.i.d. draws from the distribution with p.d.f. $p(\boldsymbol{z})$ and c.d.f. $P(\boldsymbol{z})$.

(1) Using a Gaussian kernel with standard deviation c, compute the approximations

$$\left.\begin{aligned} p_i(z_i) &= c^{-1}\frac{1}{M}\sum_{m=1}^{M}\phi\left(\frac{z_i - z_i^{(m)}}{c}\right), \\ P_i(z_i) &= \frac{1}{M}\sum_{m=1}^{M}\Phi\left(\frac{z_i - z_i^{(m)}}{c}\right) \end{aligned}\right\} \tag{3.24}$$

for $i = 1, \dots, q$. Compute this approximation at each sampled point: that is, take $z_i = z_i^{(m)}$ $(m = 1, \dots, M)$

in (3.24). This is the computationally intensive part of the algorithm.

(2) Using this approximation, transform the sampled $z_i^{(m)}$ to normally distributed $w_i^{(m)}$,

$$w_i^{(m)} = f_i(z_i^{(m)}),$$

where $f_i(\cdot) = \Phi^{-1}[P_i(\cdot)]$, and define

$$\boldsymbol{w}^{(m)} = (w_1^{(m)}, \dots, w_q^{(m)}) \quad (m = 1, \dots, M).$$

(3) The mean vector $M^{-1}\sum_{m=1}^{M} \boldsymbol{w}^{(m)} \approxeq \mathbf{0}$. Approximate the variance as the $q \times q$ matrix

$$\boldsymbol{\Sigma} = \frac{1}{M}\sum_{m=1}^{M} \boldsymbol{w}^{(m)}\boldsymbol{w}^{(m)\prime}.$$

(4) Find

$$w_i^o = f_i(z_i^o), f_i'(z_i^o) \quad (i = 1, \dots, q).$$

(5) Finally, determine

$$p(\boldsymbol{z}^o) = \phi(\boldsymbol{w}^o; \mathbf{0}, \boldsymbol{\Sigma}) \cdot \prod_{i=1}^{q} f_i'(z_i^o).$$

Densities like the ones shown in figures 3.9 and 3.11 are produced using this algorithm. Rather than evaluate the densities at a single point $\boldsymbol{z}^o$, the evaluation takes place on an appropriate grid of points, for subsequent input into standard mathematical applications software that produces contours of the form shown in those figures.

4

Incomplete Structural Models

The dynamic stochastic general equilibrium (DSGE) model has become a central analytical tool in studying aspects of economic behavior in which aggregate uncertainty is important. Models in this family abstract sufficiently from measured economic behavior that clarification of the dimensions of reality they are intended to mimic is important. This clarification is essential if these models are to deepen our understanding of real economies. If the relation between DSGE models and measured economic behavior can be made formal, explicit, and simple, then the analytic power of this approach and the understanding of economic behavior will be enhanced. This chapter explores such a characterization of the relation between DSGE models and measured economic behavior.

The approach taken here is to examine three alternative interpretations of the relationship. The first, called the strong econometric interpretation, leads to complete econometric models. It is widely understood that DSGE models fare badly under this interpretation, and the DSGE literature consistently disavows its appropriateness given the level of abstraction in the models. The second, called the weak econometric interpretation, greatly reduces the dimensions of observed behavior that a DSGE model is designed to explain. It is the interpretation advanced by Kydland and Prescott (1996). Its assumptions are in fact no weaker than those that lead to likelihood-based econometrics, and DSGE models therefore fare badly under this interpretation as well, although the failure is not so immediately evident. This chapter develops and extends a third, minimal econometric interpretation of DSGE models as being incomplete, extending work by DeJong et al. (1996). The assumptions underlying this interpretation are much weaker, and it is immune to the difficulties encountered when the DSGE model is interpreted as a complete model. To be capable of explaining measured aggregate economic behavior, however, DSGE models must, under this interpretation, be married to incomplete econometric models that provide empirically plausible descriptions of measured behavior. This chapter shows how to do this in a way that is formal, explicit, simple, and easy to implement.

The three econometric interpretations are all presented with reference to a particular substantive application: DSGE models designed to explain the equity premium. The chapter begins, in section 4.1, by setting forth four such models. The alternative econometric interpretations are taken up in turn in sections 4.2, 4.3, and 4.4. In each case numerical and graphical methods are used to illustrate the application to equity premium models. The weak econometric interpretation (section 4.3) corroborates the findings of the DSGE literature regarding the equity premium puzzle—as it must, for this is the interpretation used there. The minimal econometric interpretation (section 4.4) overturns some of the findings widely regarded as established by DSGE models.

4.1 The Essential Elements of DSGE Models

DSGE models have several common elements. They specify the preferences of economic agents over alternative paths of consumption, the technology of production, and perhaps a government sector. They assume that all economic agents choose their most preferred path of consumption. They allow stochastic perturbations to the production technology. They use the principle of competition to determine equilibrium paths of quantities and prices as functions of tastes, technology, and stochastic shocks. The specification of tastes and technology transforms the shock distribution to a distribution of quantities and prices.

The notation introduced in chapter 2 isolates the econometrically relevant implications of these models. Let A denote the assumptions of a particular model. Examples of these assumptions include the specification that preferences are time separable with constant relative risk aversion in each period, that production is Cobb-Douglas, that shocks to technology are log-normal and first-order autoregressive, and that equilibrium is competitive. Let $\boldsymbol{\theta}_A$ denote the vector of parameters that provides quantitative content for the model: for example, the specification that labor's share of income is 0.70, that the coefficient of relative risk aversion is 2.0, and so on. Finally, let "$\boldsymbol{y}$" denote an observable, finite sequence of quantities and prices whose equilibrium values the model describes: for example, ninety years of annual asset returns and output growth.

If the model has a unique equilibrium then it implies a distribution of $\boldsymbol{y}$, given the values of the parameters. The generic expression for this distribution that was introduced in chapter 2 is $p(\boldsymbol{y} \mid \boldsymbol{\theta}_A, A)$. In most DSGE models, $p(\boldsymbol{y} \mid \boldsymbol{\theta}_A, A)$ cannot be derived in closed form. As discussed in section 2.4.1 it is typically not difficult to learn about $p(\boldsymbol{y} \mid \boldsymbol{\theta}_A, A)$ by means of forward simulations: given a value of $\boldsymbol{\theta}_A$, pseudorandom vectors $\boldsymbol{y}^{(m)}$ can be drawn independently and repeatedly from $p(\boldsymbol{y} \mid \boldsymbol{\theta}_A, A)$. In many cases, this ability to simulate is sufficient to draw formal conclusions about the model and to use it to study the substantive questions it was designed to address.

4.1.1 An Example: General Equilibrium Models of the Equity Premium

Average annual real returns on relatively risk-free short-term securities in the United States have been about 1% during the past hundred years. Annual real returns on equities over the same period have averaged above 6%. The equity premium—the difference between the return to equities and the return to relatively risk-free short-term securities—has therefore exceeded 5%. Many simple general equilibrium models predict average returns on risk-free assets that are much higher than the observed average value, and average equity premia that are much lower, given parameter values generally regarded as reasonable. This predictive failure has become known as the equity premium puzzle. Kocherlakota (1996) provides a review of the literature.

In the simplest general equilibrium model of the equity premium there is a single perishable good produced and consumed each period. Let period-t production of the good be y_t, and denote the period-to-period gross growth rate of output by $x_t = y_t / y_{t-1}$.

The representative agent orders preferences over random paths of consumption $\{y_t\}$ by

$$\mathrm{E}_t\left[\sum_{s=0}^{\infty} \delta^s U(y_{t+s})\right]. \tag{4.1}$$

In this expression $\delta \in (0,1)$ is the subjective discount factor and E_t denotes expectation conditional on time-t information. The instantaneous utility function is the constant relative risk aversion (CRRA) utility function

$$U(y_t) = y_t^{1-\alpha}/(1-\alpha), \tag{4.2}$$

it being understood that $U(y_t) = \log(y_t)$ when $\alpha = 1$. The parameter α is the coefficient of relative risk aversion in the instantaneous utility function (4.2), and it is also proportional to the marginal rate of intertemporal substitution in the preference ordering (4.1).

Define a risk-free asset to be a claim to one unit of consumption in the next period. If such an asset is held in this economy, its period-t price must be

$$p_t = \delta E[U'(y_{t+1})/U'(y_t)] = \delta E_t(x_{t+1}^{-\alpha}). \tag{4.3}$$

Define one share of equity to be a claim to the fraction f of output in all future periods. If this asset is held in this economy, its period-t price must be

$$\begin{aligned} q_t &= f \cdot \mathrm{E}_t\left[\sum_{s=1}^{\infty} \frac{\delta^s U'(y_{t+s})y_{t+s}}{U'(y_t)}\right] \\ &= f y_t \mathrm{E}_t\left[\sum_{s=1}^{\infty} \frac{\delta^s U'(y_{t+s})y_{t+s}}{U'(y_t)y_t}\right] \\ &= f y_t \mathrm{E}_t\left[\sum_{s=1}^{\infty} \delta^s \prod_{j=1}^{s} x_{t+j}^{1-\alpha}\right], \end{aligned} \tag{4.4}$$

from which it follows that

$$\begin{aligned} q_t &= \delta E_t\left[\frac{U'(y_{t+1})(f y_{t+1} + q_{t+1})}{U'(y_t)}\right] \\ &= \delta E_t[x_{t+1}^{-\alpha}(f y_{t+1} + q_{t+1})]. \end{aligned} \tag{4.5}$$

From (4.4), the share price is proportional to output. If the growth rate x_t is stationary, then q_t/y_t is also stationary even though output y_t is not. This is a consequence of the assumption that instantaneous utility is of the CRRA form (4.2); in fact, (4.2) is the unique instantaneous utility function with this property in (4.1) (King et al. 1990).

4.1.2 The Mehra–Prescott and Rietz Models

Mehra and Prescott (1985) assume that the growth rate x_t is a first-order Markov chain with n discrete states. The growth rate is λ_j in state j. Assume that the time-t information set includes the history of growth rates, and let P_t denote probability conditional on time-t information. Then the Mehra–Prescott assumption can be expressed as

$$P_t(x_{t+1} = \lambda_j \mid x_t = \lambda_i) = \phi_{ij}. \tag{4.6}$$

Suppose that this economy is in state i at time t. Then, from (4.3) and (4.6), the price of the risk-free asset is

$$p_t = p^{(i)} = \delta \sum_{j=1}^{n} \phi_{ij}\lambda_j^{-\alpha},$$

and the return to the risk-free asset held from period t to period $t+1$ is

$$r_{t+1} = r^{(i)} = 1/p^{(i)} - 1.$$

From (4.4) the share price q_t is proportional to output y_t. Hence for $x_t = \lambda_i$, express the share price as $q_t = w_i y_t$. Substituting in (4.5),

$$\begin{aligned} w_i &= \delta \sum_{j=1}^{n} \phi_{ij} \lambda_j^{-\alpha} (f\lambda_j + w_j \lambda_j) \\ &= \delta \sum_{j=1}^{n} \phi_{ij} \lambda_j^{(1-\alpha)} (f + w_j) \quad (i = 1, \dots, n). \end{aligned}$$

Solving this system of n linear equations for $(w_1, \dots, w_n)$ yields the share prices $w_i y_t$. If $x_{t-1} = \lambda_i$ and $x_t = \lambda_j$, then the net return to equity holding from period $t - 1$ to period t is

$$\begin{aligned} s_t &= s^{(i,j)} \\ &= \frac{q_t + f y_t - q_{t-1}}{q_{t-1}} \\ &= \frac{w_j y_t + f y_{t-1} \lambda_j - w_i y_{t-1}}{w_i y_{t-1}} \\ &= \frac{\lambda_j (w_j + f)}{w_i} - 1. \end{aligned}$$

Mehra and Prescott (1985) take up the case $n = 2$ and impose the restriction $\phi_{11} = \phi_{22} = \phi$. They choose $\lambda_1 = 1.054$, $\lambda_2 = 0.982$, and $\phi = 0.43$ to match the mean, standard deviation, and first-order autocorrelation in the annual growth rate of per capita U.S. real consumption between 1889 and 1978. They then examine whether there are values of α less than 10 and any values of $\delta \in (0, 1)$ that are consistent with the observed average annual real returns of 0.0080 for short-term relatively risk-free assets and 0.0698 for the Standard & Poor's Composite Stock Price Index over the same period. Their conclusion is negative.

Rietz (1988) uses the same model but adds a third state for output growth ($n = 3$). The third state occurs with low probability, the growth rate in this state is quite negative, and return to one of the two normal growth states occurs with certainty in the next period. Rietz concludes that this model is consistent with the observed average returns to risk-free assets and the Stock Price Index, for some combinations of the parameter values: for example, α in the range of 5–7, δ above 0.98, and a probability of about 0.1% of a growth rate in which half of output is lost.

4.1.3 The Labadie and Tsionas Models

Labadie (1989) takes

$$\log x_t = \beta_0 + \beta_1 \log x_{t-1} + \varepsilon_t, \qquad \varepsilon_t \overset{\text{i.i.d.}}{\sim} N(0, \sigma^2).$$

Tsionas (2005) generalizes this to

$$\log x_t = \beta_0 + \beta_1 \log x_{t-1} + \omega_t^{1/2} \varepsilon_t,$$
$$\varepsilon_t \overset{\text{i.i.d.}}{\sim} N(0, 1), \qquad \omega_t \overset{\text{i.i.d.}}{\sim} p_\omega(\cdot),$$

with $\{\omega_t\}$ and $\{\varepsilon_t\}$ mutually independent. The risk-free asset price follows from (4.3):

$$\begin{aligned} p_t &= \delta E_t(x_{t+1}^{-\alpha}) \\ &= \delta \exp[-\alpha(\beta_0 + \beta_1 \log x_t)] \mathrm{E}_t[\exp(-\alpha \omega_{t+1}^{1/2} \varepsilon_{T+1})] \\ &= \delta \exp(-\alpha\beta_0) x_t^{-\alpha\beta_1} \mathrm{E}_t(\alpha^2 \omega_{t+1}/2) \\ &= \delta \exp(-\alpha\beta_0) x_t^{-\alpha\beta_1} M(\alpha^2/2), \end{aligned}$$

where $M(\cdot)$ denotes the moment-generating function of ω, $M(t) = \mathrm{E}[\exp(\omega t)]$. The net return on holding the risk-free asset is thus

$$r_t = \exp(\alpha\beta_0) x_t^{\alpha\beta_1} / \delta M(\alpha^2/2) - 1. \qquad (4.7)$$

Direct substitution in (4.4) leads to

$$q_t / f y_t = \sum_{s=1}^{\infty} c_s m_s x_t^{\alpha_s}, \tag{4.8}$$

with

$$\alpha_s = \frac{\rho\beta_1(1 - \beta_1^s)}{1 - \beta_1},$$

$$c_s = \exp\left[\frac{\rho s \beta_0}{1 - \beta_1} - \frac{\rho\beta_0\beta_1(1 - \beta_1^s)}{(1 - \beta_1)^2}\right],$$

$$m_s = \delta^s \prod_{j=1}^{s} M\left[\frac{\rho^2(1 - \beta_1^j)^2}{2(1 - \beta_1)^2}\right],$$

where $\rho = 1 - \alpha$. The expression (4.8) converges, and equilibrium with finite equity prices exists, if and only if $M[\rho^2/2(1 - \beta_1^2)] < \delta^{-1}$. Defining the left-hand side of (4.8) to be h_t, the return to equity is then $s_t = x_t(h_t + 1)/h_{t-1} - 1$.

Tsionas (2005) thus extends Labadie (1989) by permitting the growth shock to be a scale mixture of normals. The best-known scale mixture of normals is the Student-t distribution, corresponding to an inverted gamma mixing distribution $p_\omega(\cdot)$. However, the inverted gamma distribution has no moment-generating function: the implicit integral on the left-hand side of (4.7) diverges, and there is no equilibrium with finite asset prices (Geweke 2001). An attractive flexible family of symmetric distributions is the finite scale mixture of normals, for which the moment-generating function is trivial and always exists. A distribution in this family has n components, with component i assigned probability p_i. Conditional on component i, $\omega_t = \omega_{(i)}$ $(i = 1, \dots, n)$. Thus, the p.d.f. of

$u_t = \omega_t^{1/2} \varepsilon_t$ is

$$p(u_t) = (2\pi)^{-1/2} \sum_{i=1}^{n} p_i \omega_{(i)}^{-1/2} \exp(-u_t^2 / 2\omega_{(i)}).$$

To extend Labadie's model in much the same way that Rietz extended Mehra and Prescott's, let $n = 2$, let $i = 1$ denote the "normal" state, let $i = 2$ denote the "high-variance" state, and refer to the resulting specification as the Tsionas model.

The Labadie and Tsionas models can be calibrated in the same way as the Mehra–Prescott and Rietz models. In the Labadie model choose β_0, β_1, and σ^2 to match the same three moments used by Mehra and Prescott: the mean, the standard deviation, and the first-order autocorrelation coefficient of U.S. consumption growth for 1889–1978. Do the same thing for the Tsionas model, but instead substitute $\omega_{(1)}$ for σ^2. To parallel the treatment of Rietz, let $p_1 = 0.99$ and $p_2 = 0.01$ in the Tsionas model.

4.2 Strong Econometric Interpretation

Under the strong econometric interpretation a DSGE model provides a predictive distribution for an observable sequence of quantities and/or prices $\boldsymbol{y}$. Given the parameter values, $p(\boldsymbol{y} \mid \boldsymbol{\theta}_A, A)$ is the ex ante, predictive distribution for the observables $\boldsymbol{y}$. Then, letting $\boldsymbol{y}^o$ denote the observed value of $\boldsymbol{y}$, $L(\boldsymbol{\theta}_A; \boldsymbol{y}^o, A) = p(\boldsymbol{y}^o \mid \boldsymbol{\theta}_A, A)$ is the likelihood function ex post. To provide such a predictive distribution the model must specify values of the parameters $\boldsymbol{\theta}_A$, or indicate a reasonable range for parameter values and a distribution over that range, not just a distribution conditional on an unknown parameter vector $\boldsymbol{\theta}_A$. Many studies that

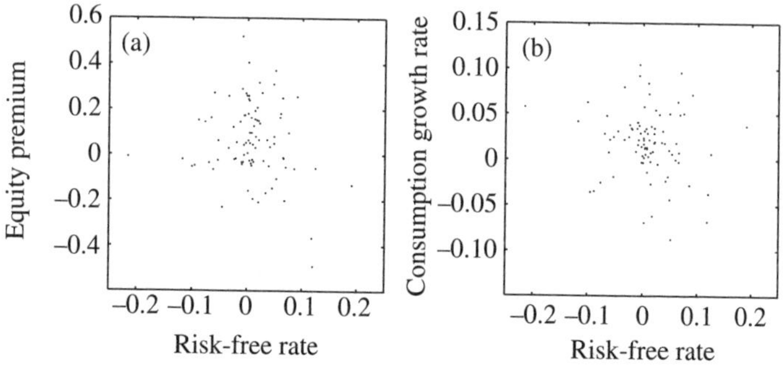

Figure 4.1. Annual combinations of (a) the risk-free rate and the equity premium and (b) the risk-free rate and the consumption growth rate, 1889–1978.

construct and calibrate DSGE models provide this sort of information about parameter values, at least informally, by means of reference to values in the literature and through their choice of calibrated values used in simulations.

In the Mehra–Prescott and Rietz variants of the DSGE equity premium models, the number of states is finite. Given n states, there can be at most n^2 different observable combinations of consumption growth and asset returns. This property obviously does not characterize the data in any literal way. Formally, the likelihood function is zero for all parameter values in these models, which would therefore be rejected by conventional econometric specification tests. In fact, the observed combinations of the risk-free rate and the equity premium have a very dispersed support, as illustrated in figure 4.1(a).

Similar problems with respect to the support of the distribution of observables arise in the Labadie and Tsionas variants of the model. Corresponding to any growth rate there is exactly one risk-free return (4.7), and to any two successive growth rates, one risky return based on (4.8). Thus, for example, these models imply that

$$\min_{(b_0,b_1,b_2)} \sum_{t=1}^{T} (r_t - b_0 - b_1 x_t^{b_2})^2 = 0. \qquad (4.9)$$

Because this condition is violated in the data, likelihood-based specification tests will reject the model. The observed combinations of growth rates and risk-free rates, displayed in figure 4.1(b), do not even suggest a relationship like (4.9).

The restriction of observables to a degenerate space of lower dimension is a well-documented failure of most DSGE models. Watson (1993), for example, has illustrated that the reduction in dimension is not even approximately true as a characterization of the data in the one-sector neoclassical model of King et al. (1988). The problem derives from the small number of shocks—often just one, as is the case here—and the larger number of observables. Smith (1993) presents a simple real business cycle model with two shocks and two observables, and employs a formal, likelihood-based approach to make inferences about parameter values. Since observables are not restricted to a space of lower dimension, his model is not trivially rejected under the strong econometric interpretation. The difficulty lies not in the economics of dynamic general equilibrium, but in developing these models to the point of accommodating a sufficiently large number of shocks in a credible way. A strong econometric interpretation of DSGE models requires an explicit accounting for the dimensions of variation observed in the data, which are not accounted for in the model.

4.3 Weak Econometric Interpretation

Most macroeconomists who work with DSGE models eschew the strong econometric interpretation. For example, Mehra and Prescott (1985), in constructing their model of consumption growth, the risk-free return, and the equity premium, plainly state that the model is intended to explain the first moments in returns but not the second moments. That is, the model purports to account for sample average values of the risk-free return and the equity premium, but not for the volatility in returns (Mehra and Prescott 1985, p. 146). Kydland and Prescott (1996, p. 69) also emphasize that the model economy is intended to "mimic the world along a carefully specified set of dimensions."

To begin the process of formalizing this interpretation of DSGE models, let $\boldsymbol{z} = f(\boldsymbol{y})$ denote the dimensions of the model that are intended to mimic the real world. In the DSGE literature such dimensions are typically sample moments: means, variances, autocorrelations, and the like. The weak econometric interpretation of a DSGE model is that the model provides a predictive distribution for the functions $\boldsymbol{z} = f(\boldsymbol{y})$ of the observable, finite sequences of quantities and/or prices $\boldsymbol{y}$. This section argues that this is the interpretation most frequently given to DSGE models by macroeconomists, including Kydland and Prescott (1996), and that it is in fact a special case of prior predictive analysis, described in section 2.4.1 and articulated at least as early as Box (1980). While applications of DSGE models sometimes resort to ad hoc comparison of predictive distributions with observed behavior, careful investigators, including Kydland and Prescott (1996), use the weak econometric interpretation of DSGE models presented here. This section illustrates this interpretation in the context of the equity premium model introduced in section 4.1. Finally, this section shows that this implementation of the weak econometric interpretation in fact makes the same assumptions as the strong econometric interpretation.

4.3.1 Formalizing the Weak Econometric Interpretation

Given a complete, probabilistic specification of the model, $p(\boldsymbol{z} \mid \boldsymbol{\theta}_A, A)$ is implied by $p(\boldsymbol{y} \mid \boldsymbol{\theta}_A, A)$ and $\boldsymbol{z} = f(\boldsymbol{y})$. Hence there is a predictive density

$$p(\boldsymbol{z} \mid A) = \int_{\Theta_A} p(\boldsymbol{\theta}_A \mid A) p(\boldsymbol{z} \mid \boldsymbol{\theta}_A, A) \, \mathrm{d}\boldsymbol{\theta}_A$$

for $\boldsymbol{z}$. Thus, from a formal econometric perspective, the dimensions of the model that are intended to mimic the real world are the functions of interest introduced in section 2.4.1.

In the DSGE literature, this predictive density is typically investigated by means of simulation. Often, $\boldsymbol{\theta}_A$ is fixed, or a few different values of $\boldsymbol{\theta}_A$ are considered to allow for uncertainty about $\boldsymbol{\theta}_A$. These are simply particular forms of the prior density $p(\boldsymbol{\theta}_A \mid A)$. Formally, the simulations in this literature take the form

$$\begin{aligned}
\boldsymbol{\theta}_A^{(m)} &\sim p(\boldsymbol{\theta}_A \mid A), \\
\boldsymbol{y}^{(m)} &\sim p(\boldsymbol{y} \mid \boldsymbol{\theta}_A^{(m)}, A), \\
\boldsymbol{z}^{(m)} &= f(\boldsymbol{y}^{(m)})
\end{aligned}$$

for $m = 1, \dots, M$. As discussed in section 3.2, the pseudorandom vectors $\boldsymbol{z}^{(m)}$ characterize the predictive distribution of the model and can be compared with the observed value, $\boldsymbol{z}^o$.

Kydland and Prescott (1996, p. 70) are quite clear about this process:

> If the model has aggregate uncertainty ... then the model will imply a process governing the random evolution of the economy. In the case of uncertainty, the computer can generate any number of independent realizations of the equilibrium stochastic process, and these relations, along with statistical estimation theory, are then used to measure the sampling distribution of any desired set of statistics of the model economy.

And again (Kydland and Prescott 1996, pp. 75–76):

> If the model economy has aggregate uncertainty, first a set of statistics that summarize relevant aspects of the behavior of the actual economy is selected. Then the computational experiment is used to generate many independent realizations of the equilibrium process for the model economy. In this way, the sampling distribution of this set of statistics can be determined to any degree of accuracy for the model economy and compared with the values of the set of statistics for the actual economy. In comparing the sampling distribution of a statistic for the model economy to the value of that statistic for the actual data, it is crucial that the same statistic be computed for the model and the real world. If, for example, the statistic for the real world is for a 50-year period, then the statistic for the model economy must also be for a 50-year period.

A formal Bayesian approach conditions on $\boldsymbol{z}^o$: the observed dimensions of the real world the model is intended to address. Given two competing models, A and B, the posterior odds ratio is then

$$\frac{p(A \mid \boldsymbol{z}^o)}{p(B \mid \boldsymbol{z}^o)} = \frac{p(A)p(\boldsymbol{z}^o \mid A)}{p(B)p(\boldsymbol{z}^o \mid B)}.$$

For the purposes of model evaluation and comparison, therefore, it is the predictive density of $\mathbf{z}$ at the observed value $\mathbf{z}^o$ that matters. This has long been recognized in the Bayesian model evaluation literature, as discussed in section 2.4.1. Lancaster (2004, p. 81) has noted that calibration as conventionally practiced is a special case of prior predictive analysis.

If the order of the vector $\mathbf{z}$ is not too large, then numerical approximation of $p(\mathbf{z}^o \mid A)$ is straightforward and much simpler than numerical approximation of the full marginal likelihoods would be under the strong econometric interpretation of the DSGE model. The latter requires backward simulation, for example by means of a Markov chain Monte Carlo algorithm. The former only requires the $\mathbf{z}^{(m)}$ produced through the forward simulations reported in the DSGE literature. Conventional smoothing procedures like kernel density methods will provide a numerical approximation to $p(\mathbf{z}^o \mid A)$:

$$p(\mathbf{z}^o \mid A) \approxeq M^{-1} \sum_{m=1}^{M} K(\mathbf{z}^{(m)}; \mathbf{z}^o),$$

where the kernel smoother $K(\mathbf{z}; \mathbf{z}^o)$ is a nonnegative function of $\mathbf{z}$ that is concentrated near $\mathbf{z}^o$ and integrates to one.

4.3.2 Illustration in the Equity Premium Model

The Mehra–Prescott and Labadie models completely specify the distribution of growth. The Rietz and Tsionas models each specify the distribution of growth up to a single, unknown parameter: λ_3, growth in the event of a crash, and $\omega_{(2)}$, the high variance, respectively. For the Rietz model, adopt the prior

Table 4.1. Deciles of prior distributions.

Decile	λ_3	$\omega_{(2)}$	α	δ
0.1	0.185	0.332	0.281	0.840
0.2	0.277	0.491	0.499	0.907
0.3	0.358	0.677	0.756	0.939
0.4	0.434	0.917	1.077	0.958
0.5	0.509	1.26	1.500	0.970
0.6	0.583	1.77	2.089	0.979
0.7	0.659	2.68	2.978	0.986
0.8	0.738	4.61	4.509	0.991
0.9	0.826	11.12	8.016	0.995

distribution

$$\log[\lambda_3/(1-\lambda_3)] \sim N(0.036, 1.185^2);$$

and for the Tsionas model, use

$$1.33/\omega_{(2)} \sim \chi^2(1.66).$$

Deciles for both distributions are given in table 4.1. The distribution of λ_3 is centered at $\lambda_3 = 0.509$, halving of expected output, which is the intermediate of the three examples taken up in Rietz (1988). The distribution of $\omega_{(2)}$ centers the standard deviation in the high-variance state about 1.26, implying that in this state output is about as likely to be between one-third and triple its normal value as it is to be outside this range.

All other parameters in the models pertain to the consumption growth process. In the exercises reported here these parameters were held fixed at their calibrated values, which are chosen to reproduce the mean, standard deviation, and first-order autocorrelation of the consumption growth rate. Modifying the analysis by introducing prior distributions for these parameters increases the technical complexity of the exercise, because the dimension of the predictive distribution is increased from two to five, but should have little effect on the final results.

None of the models fix the relative risk aversion parameter α or the subjective rate of discount δ. This analysis employs priors that should provide substantial probabilities over the ranges most economists would regard as plausible. For α, take

$$\log \alpha \sim N(0.4055, 1.3077^2),$$

and for δ,

$$\log[\delta/(1-\delta)] \sim N(3.476, 1.418^2).$$

Deciles for these prior distributions are also shown in table 4.1. The prior distribution for α is centered at $\alpha = 1.5$, and a centered 80% prior credible interval for α is $(0.281, 8.016)$. The prior distribution for δ is centered at 0.97, and a centered 80% prior credible interval is $(0.840, 0.995)$.

These prior distributions, together with the data densities described in section 4.1, provide predictive densities for all four models. For each model, draws from predictive densities for output growth rate and asset returns can be made by

(1) drawing from the prior distributions of the unknown parameters;

(2) conditional on the drawn parameters, generating a sample of ninety successive years of growth rates from the probability density for $\{x_t\}$; and

(3) solving for the risk-free and risky returns in each year as indicated in section 4.1.

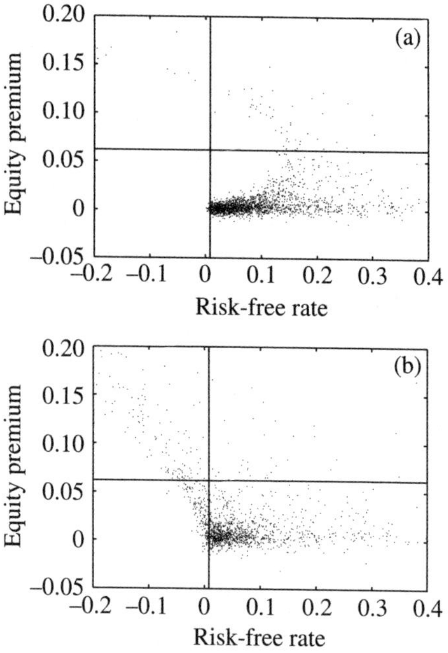

Figure 4.2. Predictive distributions for the risk-free rate and the equity premium under the weak econometric interpretation. (a) The Mehra–Prescott model. (b) The Rietz model.

Draws from the predictive density for any function of output growth rate and asset returns are then just the corresponding functions of this generated, synthetic sample. For example, to draw from the predictive density for ninety-year means of the risk-free rate and the equity premium, following step (3) just construct these functions and record them. Notice that the predictive density for the mean risk-free rate and the mean equity premium accounts for both uncertainty about parameter values (by means of the draws from the prior) and sampling variation due to

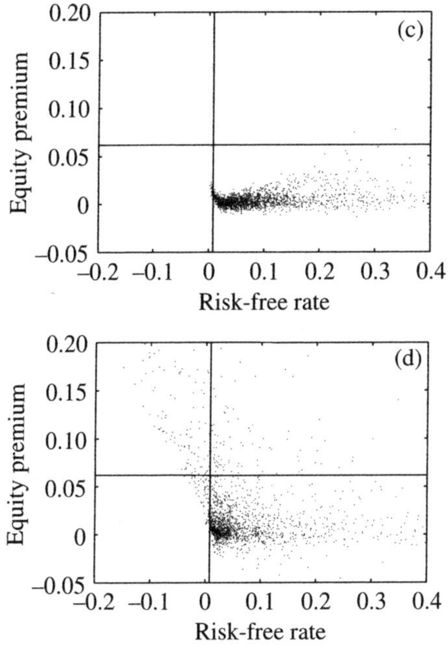

Figure 4.2. (*Continued.*) (c) The Labadie model. (d) The Tsionas model.

ninety-year averaging (by means of the ninety-year simulation).

Figure 4.2 shows the predictive distributions for ninety-year averages of the risk-free return and the equity premium, as represented by 1,000 points $\tilde{\boldsymbol{z}}^{(m)}$ drawn from $p(\boldsymbol{z} \mid A)$ for each model. In each panel, the vertical line indicates the observed value of 0.008 for the risk-free rate and the horizontal line indicates the observed value of 0.0618 for the equity premium. The supports of the Rietz and Tsionas model predictive distributions include the observed values, but those of the Mehra–Prescott and Labadie model predictive densities do not. This corroborates the failure of the latter two models to explain the equity premium puzzle in the weak econometric DSGE literature, and the ability of the Rietz and Tsionas models to account for the observed means.

High values of the risk-free rate correspond to low values of δ. Negative values of the risk-free rate and high equity premia in the Rietz and Tsionas models typically reflect high risk aversion in conjunction with a low probability of very negative growth rates. The values of the risk-free rate and the equity premium in the Rietz and Tsionas models close to the historical averages typically correspond to situations in which very negative growth rates were possible but did not occur during the simulated ninety-year history.

Table 4.2 provides approximations of the log prior predictive density, $\log[p(\mathbf{z}^o \mid A)]$, of each of the four models under the weak econometric interpretation. An independent symmetric bivariate Gaussian density kernel was centered at the observed sample mean for the risk-free return and the equity premium, and points were drawn from the predictive density $p(\mathbf{z} \mid A)$. Various standard deviations were used as indicated in the left-hand column of table 4.2. As one moves down the rows, approximations show greater bias (because they include values of $\mathbf{z}^{(m)}$ farther from the data point) but less variance (because more points are given weight). Asymptotic standard errors for the kernel density approximations are indicated parenthetically. Table 4.2 shows that the prior predictive densities of the Mehra–Prescott and Labadie models are zero at the observed value $\mathbf{z}^o$. The Tsionas model is favored over the Rietz model, the Bayes factor being about 3:1.

Table 4.2. Weak econometric interpretation: Relative log marginal likelihoods.

Gaussian smoothing kernel standard deviation	Model (random draws)			
	Mehra-Prescott (10^8)	Rietz (10^8)	Labadie (10^6)	Tsionas (10^6)
0.0001	$-\infty$	1.512 (0.011)	$-\infty$	3.04 (0.76)
0.0003	$-\infty$	1.887 (0.036)	$-\infty$	2.90 (0.21)
0.0010	−114	1.902 (0.011)	−455	3.07 (0.06)
0.0030	−19.03 (0.39)	1.9228 (0.0036)	−53.72 (0.68)	3.01 (0.02)
0.0100	−3.0153 (0.0006)	2.1558 (0.0009)	−2.894 (0.004)	3.086 (0.006)

The numerical standard error of the kernel approximation is indicated parenthetically for table entries.

4.3.3 Difficulties with the Weak Econometric Interpretation

As the DSGE literature emphasizes, all models are approximations of reality, and it is important to clarify which aspects of reality a model is intended to mimic. In the strong econometric interpretation of a model, this limited scope is recognized in the choice of the random vector $\boldsymbol{y}$. If, subsequently, attention is shifted to only a subset of the original variables, there are no conceptual difficulties: one simply works with the marginal distributions of the included variables.

The dimensions of reality addressed by DSGE models entail a limitation in scope of a different kind. For example, the equity premium models are intended to explain sample means of the risk-free return and the equity premium, but no other aspects of these returns. This is not possible: if the model accounts for $(T+1)$-year averages as well as T-year averages, then the model also has implications for the year-to-year returns.

More significantly, the DSGE calibration literature takes the short-run dynamics of these models literally, in establishing the sampling distribution of the set of statistics $\boldsymbol{z}$ that summarize the relevant aspects of the behavior of the actual economy. This fact is emphasized in Kydland and Prescott (1996). It is made quite clear in careful calibration studies: see, for example, Gregory and Smith (1991, p. 298) and Christiano and Eichenbaum (1992, pp. 436, 439). Bayesian prior predictive analysis of a complete model also incorporates all of the dynamics of the model, and the use of the sampling distribution of $\boldsymbol{z}$ in the DSGE calibration literature is equivalent to such an analysis.

There is an important distinction in context between the DSGE calibration literature and a prior predictive analysis, however. The latter treats the model as descriptive of the entire distribution of $\boldsymbol{z}$. The former regards the model as predictive for the first moment but for no other aspects of $\boldsymbol{z}$. The sampling distribution of the statistic $\boldsymbol{z}$ is often a function of profoundly unrealistic aspects of DSGE models, aspects that lie outside the dimensions of reality that the models were intended to mimic. For example, in the equity premium models, the sampling distribution of average asset returns over the ninety-year period are closely related to the variances of these returns, through the usual arithmetic for the standard deviation of a sample mean. In establishing the sampling distribution of these means through repeated simulation of the model, one is taking literally the second moments of returns inherent in the model. These are precisely the dimensions the original model was not intended to capture (Mehra and Prescott 1985, p. 146), and the models are unrealistic in these dimensions. For example, the sample standard deviation of the equity premium is 0.164 in the 1889–1979 data, whereas at prior median values the standard deviation is 0.055 in the Mehra–Prescott model and 0.258 in the Rietz model.

The weak econometric interpretation of DSGE models leads to formal methods for model comparison that are easy to implement and have an unambiguous interpretation. As a by-product, there are some interesting and useful visual displays. But the assumptions that underlie the weak econometric interpretation are in fact the same as those made in the strong econometric interpretation: the model is assumed to account for all aspects of the observed sequence of quantities and/or prices.

4.4 Minimal Econometric Interpretation

The logical problems encountered in the proposition that DSGE models account for only a few sample moments of observed sequences of quantities and prices prevents the development of this notion into coherent methods of inference about these models. To broaden the proposition to assert that DSGE models in fact provide likelihood functions leads to outright dismissal of many of these models. This section considers a more modest claim for DSGE models, also studied by DeJong et al. (1996): that they account only for population moments of specified, observable functions of sequences of prices and/or quantities. A DSGE model, A, with a given parameter vector $\boldsymbol{\theta}_A$ implies *population* moments $\boldsymbol{m} = \mathrm{E}(\boldsymbol{z} \mid \boldsymbol{\theta}_A, A)$, where $\boldsymbol{z} = f(\boldsymbol{y})$ is the same vector of *sample* moments considered under the weak econometric interpretation. If A is endowed with a prior distribution $p(\boldsymbol{\theta}_A \mid A)$, then A provides a distribution for $\boldsymbol{m}$ as well. But the model A does not provide a distribution for $\boldsymbol{y}$ or $\boldsymbol{z}$, and is therefore incomplete.

By not claiming to predict sample moments, the minimal econometric interpretation avoids the logical pitfall that carrying out inference based on the model's predictive distribution for these moments inevitably leads back to a conventional likelihood function. What is given up in this retreat is that the DSGE model, by itself, now has no implications for anything that might be observed—no one will ever see a population moment. To endow such a model with empirical content it is necessary to posit, separately, a link between the population moments $\boldsymbol{m}$ and the observable sequence of prices and/or quantities $\boldsymbol{y}$. DeJong et al. (1996) also noted the need for such a link. This section shows how to do this formally, and provides some examples of the procedure. The result is an integration of atheoretical econometric models with DSGE models.

4.4.1 Formal Development

Let A and B denote two alternative DSGE models, each describing the same vector of population moments $\boldsymbol{m}$ by means of the respective densities $p(\boldsymbol{m} \mid A)$ and $p(\boldsymbol{m} \mid B)$. The densities could be degenerate at a point but in general are not because of subjective uncertainty about parameter values in both models.

Introduce a third econometric model E that specifies a conditional distribution of observables $p(\boldsymbol{y} \mid$

$\boldsymbol{\theta}_E, \boldsymbol{m}, E)$ together with a proper conditional prior distribution $p(\boldsymbol{\theta}_E \mid \boldsymbol{m}, E)$. Model E is incomplete because it provides no prior distribution $p(\boldsymbol{m} \mid E)$: in this sense it may be said to be atheoretical. The prior distribution for $\boldsymbol{m}$ is provided either by model A through $p(\boldsymbol{m} \mid A)$ or by model B through $p(\boldsymbol{m} \mid B)$. Thus we have the following condition.

Condition 4.1. Conditional on the DSGE model A and the econometric model E,

$$p(\boldsymbol{m}, \boldsymbol{\theta}_E, \boldsymbol{y} \mid A, E) = p(\boldsymbol{m} \mid A) \cdot p(\boldsymbol{\theta}_E \mid \boldsymbol{m}, E) \cdot p(\boldsymbol{y} \mid \boldsymbol{\theta}_E, \boldsymbol{m}, E).$$

Conditional on the DSGE model B and the econometric model E,

$$p(\boldsymbol{m}, \boldsymbol{\theta}_E, \boldsymbol{y} \mid B, E) = p(\boldsymbol{m} \mid B) \cdot p(\boldsymbol{\theta}_E \mid \boldsymbol{m}, E) \cdot p(\boldsymbol{y} \mid \boldsymbol{\theta}_E, \boldsymbol{m}, E).$$

The sole function of the DSGE model is to provide a prior distribution for $\boldsymbol{m}$.

Proposition 4.2. *Given condition 4.1,*

$$\begin{aligned} p(\boldsymbol{y} \mid \boldsymbol{m}, A, E) &= \frac{\int p(\boldsymbol{m}, \boldsymbol{\theta}_E, \boldsymbol{y} \mid A, E)\, \mathrm{d}\boldsymbol{\theta}_E}{p(\boldsymbol{m} \mid A, E)} \\ &= \frac{\int p(\boldsymbol{m} \mid A) p(\boldsymbol{\theta}_E \mid \boldsymbol{m}, E) p(\boldsymbol{y} \mid \boldsymbol{\theta}_E, \boldsymbol{m}, E)\, \mathrm{d}\boldsymbol{\theta}_E}{p(\boldsymbol{m} \mid A)} \\ &= \int p(\boldsymbol{\theta}_E \mid \boldsymbol{m}, E) p(\boldsymbol{y} \mid \boldsymbol{\theta}_E, \boldsymbol{m}, E)\, \mathrm{d}\boldsymbol{\theta}_E \\ &= p(\boldsymbol{y} \mid \boldsymbol{m}, E), \end{aligned}$$

and $p(\boldsymbol{y} \mid \boldsymbol{m}, B, E) = p(\boldsymbol{y} \mid \boldsymbol{m}, E)$ *as well.*

Condition 4.1 and proposition 4.2 lead to the following result.

Proposition 4.3. *Given condition 4.1,*

$$\frac{p(A \mid \boldsymbol{y}^o, E)}{p(B \mid \boldsymbol{y}^o, E)} = \frac{p(A \mid E)p(\boldsymbol{y}^o \mid A, E)}{p(B \mid E)p(\boldsymbol{y}^o \mid B, E)} = \frac{p(A \mid E) \int p(\boldsymbol{m} \mid A)p(\boldsymbol{y}^o \mid \boldsymbol{m}, E)\,\mathrm{d}\boldsymbol{m}}{p(B \mid E) \int p(\boldsymbol{m} \mid B)p(\boldsymbol{y}^o \mid \boldsymbol{m}, E)\,\mathrm{d}\boldsymbol{m}}. \tag{4.10}$$

The evidence about models A and B, in the context of the econometric model E, is in the convolutions

$$\left.\begin{aligned} &\int p(\boldsymbol{m} \mid A)p(\boldsymbol{y}^o \mid \boldsymbol{m}, E)\,\mathrm{d}\boldsymbol{m}, \\ &\int p(\boldsymbol{m} \mid B)p(\boldsymbol{y}^o \mid \boldsymbol{m}, E)\,\mathrm{d}\boldsymbol{m}, \end{aligned}\right\} \tag{4.11}$$

whose ratio in (4.10) is the Bayes factor in favor of model A. Loosely speaking, if $p(\boldsymbol{y}^o \mid \boldsymbol{m}, E)$ overlaps more with $p(\boldsymbol{m} \mid A)$ than with $p(\boldsymbol{m} \mid B)$, the Bayes factor favors model A. This looser interpretation underlies the confidence interval criterion proposed in DeJong et al. (1996), for univariate m. The odds ratio (4.10) provides an exact interpretation, which also extends to multivariate $\boldsymbol{m}$.

The expression

$$\int p(\boldsymbol{m} \mid A)p(\boldsymbol{y}^o \mid \boldsymbol{m}, E)\,\mathrm{d}\boldsymbol{m}$$

in (4.11) is the convolution of two densities, the first of which is the density for $\boldsymbol{m}$ implied by the DSGE model, A. It can be accessed by means of the conventional simulations used in the calibration literature: if $\boldsymbol{\theta}_A^{(r)}$ is a random sample from $p(\boldsymbol{\theta}_A \mid A)$, then $\boldsymbol{m}_A^{(r)} = \boldsymbol{m}(\boldsymbol{\theta}_A^{(r)})$ is a random sample from $p(\boldsymbol{m} \mid A)$; similarly for $p(\boldsymbol{m} \mid B)$.

To access $p(\boldsymbol{y}^o \mid \boldsymbol{m}, E)$, the second density in (4.11), define the auxiliary model E^* with the improper prior density $p(\boldsymbol{m} \mid E^*) \propto$ constant, $p(\boldsymbol{\theta}_E \mid \boldsymbol{m}, E^*) = p(\boldsymbol{\theta}_E \mid \boldsymbol{m}, E)$, and $p(\boldsymbol{y} \mid \boldsymbol{\theta}_E, \boldsymbol{m}, E) = p(\boldsymbol{y} \mid \boldsymbol{\theta}_E, \boldsymbol{m}, E^*)$. Then

$$\begin{aligned} p(\boldsymbol{m} \mid \boldsymbol{y}^o, E^*) &\propto \int p(\boldsymbol{m} \mid E^*) p(\boldsymbol{\theta}_E \mid \boldsymbol{m}, E^*) p(\boldsymbol{y}^o \mid \boldsymbol{\theta}_E, \boldsymbol{m}, E^*) \, \mathrm{d}\boldsymbol{\theta}_E \\ &\propto \int p(\boldsymbol{\theta}_E \mid \boldsymbol{m}, E) p(\boldsymbol{y}^o \mid \boldsymbol{\theta}_E, \boldsymbol{m}, E) \, \mathrm{d}\boldsymbol{\theta}_E \\ &= p(\boldsymbol{y}^o \mid \boldsymbol{m}, E). \end{aligned} \tag{4.12}$$

A posterior simulator for $\boldsymbol{y}^o$ and the auxiliary model E^* provides a sample $\boldsymbol{m}_{E*}^{(s)}$ whose density kernel is $p(\boldsymbol{y}^o \mid \boldsymbol{m}, E)$.

Thus, from (4.10),

$$\frac{p(A \mid \boldsymbol{y}^o, E)}{p(B \mid \boldsymbol{y}^o, E)} = \frac{p(A \mid E) \int p(\boldsymbol{m} \mid A) p(\boldsymbol{m} \mid \boldsymbol{y}^o, E^*) \, \mathrm{d}\boldsymbol{m}}{p(B \mid E) \int p(\boldsymbol{m} \mid B) p(\boldsymbol{m} \mid \boldsymbol{y}^o, E^*) \, \mathrm{d}\boldsymbol{m}}.$$

Models A and B can be compared on the basis of three simulations of the moment vector $\boldsymbol{m}$:

$$\begin{aligned} &\boldsymbol{m}_A^{(r)} \ (r = 1, \dots, N_A) && \text{drawn from } p(\boldsymbol{m} \mid A), \\ &\boldsymbol{m}_B^{(r)} \ (r = 1, \dots, N_B) && \text{drawn from } p(\boldsymbol{m} \mid B), \\ &\boldsymbol{m}_{E*}^{(s)} \ (s = 1, \dots, N_{E*}) && \text{drawn from } p(\boldsymbol{m} \mid \boldsymbol{y}^o, E^*). \end{aligned}$$

Informal comparison can be based on a visual inspection of the clouds of points from these three models. A more formal comparison can be made by means of the kernel density approximation,

$$\begin{aligned} p(A \mid \boldsymbol{y}^o, E) \\ \propto p(A \mid E)(N_A N_{E*})^{-1} \sum_{r=1}^{N_A} \sum_{s=1}^{N_{E*}} K(\boldsymbol{m}_A^{(r)}, \boldsymbol{m}_{E*}^{(s)}), \end{aligned} \tag{4.13}$$

and similarly for $p(B \mid \boldsymbol{y}^o, E)$.

Table 4.3. Posterior moments in the vector autoregression (parameters defined in (4.14)).

Parameter	Mean	Standard deviation
m_1	0.0088	0.0106
m_2	0.0591	0.0227
f_{11}	0.4362	0.0907
f_{12}	−0.0972	0.0303
f_{21}	−0.0065	0.3143
f_{22}	0.2003	0.1077
σ_{11}	0.0022	0.0003
σ_{22}	0.0268	0.0041
σ_{12}	−0.0009	0.0008

4.4.2 Illustration in the Equity Premium Model

In the equity premium example the vector $\boldsymbol{m}$ consists of the population means for the risk-free rate and the equity premium. Perhaps the simplest econometric model E with implications for $\boldsymbol{m}$ is a first-order Gaussian bivariate autoregression for the risk-free rate and equity premium, with stationarity imposed:

$$\boldsymbol{y}_t - \boldsymbol{m} = \boldsymbol{F}(\boldsymbol{y}_{t-1} - \boldsymbol{m}) + \boldsymbol{\varepsilon}_t \quad (t = 1879, \dots, 1978),$$

where the 2×1 vector $\boldsymbol{y}_t$ consists of the observed risk-free rate r_t and the equity premium e_t in the indicated year, and $\boldsymbol{\varepsilon}_t \overset{\text{i.i.d.}}{\sim} N(\boldsymbol{0}, \boldsymbol{\Sigma})$.

Draws of $\boldsymbol{m}$ from the posterior distribution were obtained using a Metropolis within Gibbs posterior simulation algorithm. An improper prior for $(\boldsymbol{m}, \boldsymbol{F}, \boldsymbol{\Sigma})$, flat subject to the stationarity condition on $\boldsymbol{F}$, was employed. This prior satisfies the conditions for the model E^* discussed above. Some posterior moments for the parameters of the model

$$\left.\begin{aligned} \begin{pmatrix} r_t - m_1 \\ e_t - m_2 \end{pmatrix} &= \begin{bmatrix} f_{11} & f_{12} \\ f_{21} & f_{22} \end{bmatrix} \begin{pmatrix} r_{t-1} - m_1 \\ e_{t-1} - m_2 \end{pmatrix} + \begin{pmatrix} \varepsilon_{1t} \\ \varepsilon_{2t} \end{pmatrix}, \\ \begin{pmatrix} \varepsilon_{1t} \\ \varepsilon_{2t} \end{pmatrix} &\overset{\text{i.i.d.}}{\sim} N\left(\begin{pmatrix} 0 \\ 0 \end{pmatrix}, \begin{bmatrix} \sigma_{11} & \sigma_{12} \\ \sigma_{12} & \sigma_{22} \end{bmatrix} \right) \end{aligned}\right\} \tag{4.14}$$

are indicated in table 4.3. There is modest autocorrelation in the risk-free rate (about 0.4), less in the equity premium (about 0.2), and very little cross-correlation between the two time series. The innovation variance in the equity premium exceeds that of the risk-free rate by a factor of more than 10. The implied standard deviation for the equity premium is over 0.16, and that for the risk-free rate is over 0.05.

The posterior distribution of $\boldsymbol{m}$ is indicated by the crosses in each panel of figure 4.3. The range of values well within the support of the posterior distribution extends far beyond the observed sample means, indicated by the horizontal and vertical lines in each panel. A centered 90% posterior credible interval for the mean of the risk-free rate extends from −0.9% to 2.6%. For the equity premium the range is much larger: from 2.2% to 9.7%. Even with ninety years of data, there is great uncertainty about the population mean of the equity premium. This uncertainty is due to the great variance in the equity premium from year to year. It is not due to drift: there has been no tendency for the equity premium to rise or fall secularly (Mehra and Prescott 1985, table 1), and the autocorrelation in the simple model used here is only 0.2.

The dots in each panel of figure 4.3 represent the p.d.f. $p(\boldsymbol{m} \mid A)$ for the indicated model A. For each model, parameters were drawn from the same prior

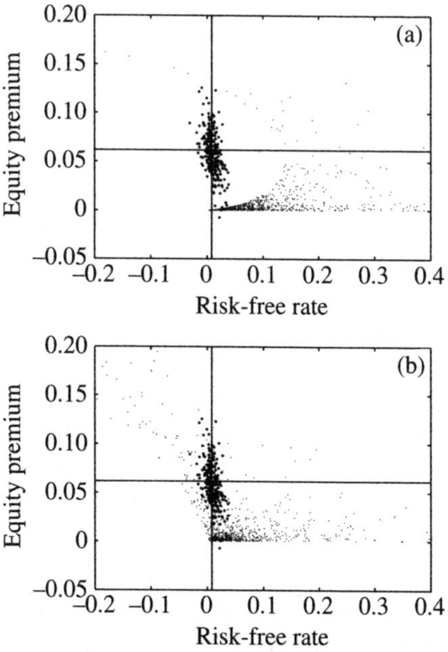

Figure 4.3. Distributions under the minimal econometric interpretation. Pluses represent the posterior distribution in the econometric model E^*. (a) The Mehra–Prescott model. (b) The Rietz model.

distributions used in the weak econometric interpretation. (These priors are summarized in table 4.1.) The corresponding population moments were then computed. For the Mehra–Prescott and Rietz models there are closed-form expressions for these moments. For the Labadie and Tsionas models, a simulation of 1,000 periods was made corresponding to each set of parameter values drawn from the prior. A second antithetic simulation (i.e., shocks with signs reversed) was then made. The mean of the risk-free rate and the equity premium averaged over the two 1,000-period

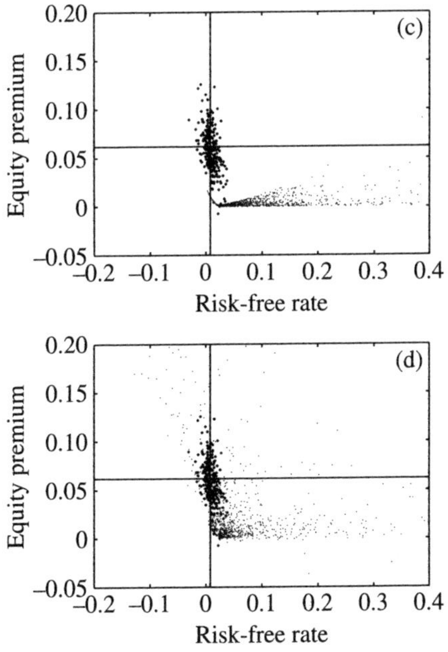

Figure 4.3. (*Continued.*) (c) The Labadie model. (d) The Tsionas model.

simulations was then used in lieu of the population mean.

Comparisons of the panels in figure 4.2 with the corresponding ones in figure 4.3 reveal similar patterns. But the distributions in figure 4.2 are more diffuse, relative to those in the latter figures, which are more neatly demarcated and somewhat more compact. The difference reflects the sampling variation in ninety-year averages, which is present in figure 4.2 but not in figure 4.3.

In the minimal econometric interpretation, a model receives support to the extent that the posterior density $p(\boldsymbol{m} \mid \boldsymbol{y}^o, E^*)$, represented by the crosses in figure 4.3, overlaps with the prior density $p(\boldsymbol{m} \mid A)$, represented by the dots, in a manner that is made explicit in expression (4.12). Because the posterior density $p(\boldsymbol{m} \mid \boldsymbol{y}^o, E)$ is so diffuse, there is substantial overlap between $p(\boldsymbol{m} \mid \boldsymbol{y}^o, E^*)$ and $p(\boldsymbol{m} \mid A)$ for each of the four alternative models A. This is true even of the Mehra–Prescott and Labadie models, which received no support under the weak econometric interpretation. The weak econometric interpretation takes literally the unrealistically small variance in the risk-free return and the equity premium implied by these two models and concludes that they cannot account for the observed averages. The minimal econometric interpretation utilizes the much greater sampling variation implied by the bivariate autoregression, and interprets the historical evidence about population moments as being much weaker. This finding underscores the point made forcefully by Eichenbaum (1991, p. 611) that assuming that the population moment is equal to the sample moment can be treacherous.

Formal approximation using (4.13) supports these informal findings: see table 4.4, which uses some of the same Gaussian kernels employed in table 4.2. The ordering by Bayes factors is Tsionas model over Rietz model over Labadie model over Mehra–Prescott model, with the ratios being roughly 5:2:1:0.55. These conclusions are robust over the bandwidths indicated in table 4.4.

4.5 Implications for Structural Modeling

This chapter examined three distinct interpretations of the implications of a structural model for observed

Table 4.4. Minimal econometric interpretation: Relative log marginal likelihoods.

Gaussian smoothing kernel standard deviation	Model			
	Mehra-Prescott	Rietz	Labadie	Mixture
0.001	1.548 (0.007)	2.825 (0.016)	2.141 (0.006)	3.709 (0.008)
0.003	1.699 (0.005)	2.837 (0.011)	2.053 (0.005)	3.696 (0.008)
0.010	1.842 (0.005)	2.928 (0.008)	2.144 (0.005)	3.629 (0.007)

Note: approximations use (4.13) with $N_A = 10^6$, $N_E^* = 10^5$. The numerical standard error of the kernel approximation is indicated parenthetically for table entries.

behavior. Since these models imply distributions for the paths of prices and quantities, a straightforward, likelihood-based approach—termed the strong econometric interpretation in this chapter—is perhaps the most obvious. Many DSGE models fail under this interpretation because they predict exact relations that are not found in the data.

A widespread interpretation of DSGE models in the macroeconomics literature is that they are intended only to mimic the world along a carefully specified set of dimensions. This interpretation is sometimes reduced to a list of sample moments, on the one hand, and a list of corresponding moments of the model's predictive distribution, on the other. Careful investigators recognize that some basis for comparison of these two sets of moments is needed. Kydland and Prescott (1996) clearly indicate that what is at stake is whether the sample moments are consistent with the predictive distribution of the model for those moments. This inherently Bayesian approach—termed the weak econometric interpretation in this chapter, and equivalent to a prior predictive analysis—takes the period-to-period dynamics of the models literally in comparing sample moments with the distribution of these sample moments implied by the DSGE model. While it confines itself to just a few dimensions of the data, in accounting for sampling variation it makes the same assumptions as the strong econometric interpretation does. It is therefore subject to the same criticism: that those assumptions are inconsistent with what is observed.

To isolate the idea that DSGE models explain only certain dimensions of the data, in a way that does not run afoul of the literal incredibility of these models, this chapter examined the implications of the claim that DSGE models predict only certain specified population moments of observable data. Since population moments are never observed, a link between population and sample moments must be forged if the DSGE model is to have refutable implications. The chapter showed that atheoretical econometric models with no claim to prior information about the population moments in question can perform this function, with the DSGE model providing the prior distribution for the dimensions it addresses. Under this set of assumptions—termed the minimal econometric interpretation—formal model comparison is possible and is free of the logical problems associated with the weak econometric interpretation. It leads to comparison of the prior distribution of the population moments that the model is intended to describe with the posterior distribution of these moments in the auxiliary econometric model.

These ideas were illustrated using the "equity premium puzzle" models of Mehra and Prescott (1985), Rietz (1988), Labadie (1989), and Tsionas (2005). The weak econometric interpretation reaffirmed both the inability of the Mehra–Prescott and Labadie models to account for the sample average risk-free rate and the equity premium in the United States, and the ability of the Rietz and Tsionas models to do so. This reflects the fact that it is the weak econometric interpretation that is dominant in the DSGE literature of macroeconomics. This application provided a rich graphical interpretation of these models as well as Bayes factors for the comparison of models.

The minimal econometric interpretation of the same models greatly changed the nature of the findings, and underscores that point that the methodological issues raised in this chapter have substantive implications for macroeconomics. The most important finding was that information about the population mean of the equity premium is limited due to its large year-to-year fluctuations. The posterior distribution for the mean of the risk-free rate and the equity premium supports values consistent with the original Mehra–Prescott model, the other models considered in this chapter, and perhaps with many other DSGE models designed to address this question as well. In the context of the minimal econometric interpretation of these models there is no evidence of an equity premium puzzle in the canonical U.S. data set used to study this question.

5
An Incomplete Model Space

The formal solutions of most decision problems in economics, in the private and public sectors as well as in academic contexts, require probability distributions for magnitudes that are as yet unknown. Point forecasts are rarely sufficient. For econometric investigators whose work may be used by clients in different situations the rationale for producing predictive distributions is clear.

Increasing awareness of these requirements, combined with advances in modeling and computing, is leading to a sustained emphasis on these distributions in econometric research (Diebold et al. 1998; Christoffersen 1998; Corradi and Swanson 2006a,b; Gneiting et al. 2007). In many situations several models with predictive distributions are available, and this naturally leads to questions of model choice or combination. While there is a large econometric literature on choice or combination of point forecasts, dating at least to Bates and Granger (1969) and extending through many subsequent contributions reviewed recently by Timmermann (2006), the treatment of predictive density combination in the econometrics literature is much more limited. Granger et al. (1989) and Clements (2006) attacked the related problems of event and quantile forecast combination, respectively.

Wallis (2005) was perhaps the first econometrician to take up combinations of predictive densities explicitly. Hall and Mitchell (2007) developed the closest precursor of the approach taken here.

5.1 Context and Motivation

This chapter considers the situation in which alternative models provide predictive distributions for a vector time series $\boldsymbol{y}_t$ given its history $\boldsymbol{Y}_{t-1} = \{\boldsymbol{y}_1, \dots, \boldsymbol{y}_{t-1}\}$. A prediction model A (for "assumptions") is a construction that produces a probability density for $\boldsymbol{y}_t$ from the history $\boldsymbol{Y}_{t-1}$ denoted $p(\boldsymbol{y}_t; \boldsymbol{Y}_{t-1}, A)$. There are many kinds of prediction models. Some important examples begin with parametric conditional densities $p(\boldsymbol{y}_t \mid \boldsymbol{Y}_{t-1}, \boldsymbol{\theta}_A, A)$. Then, in a formal Bayesian approach, the predictive density $p(\boldsymbol{y}_t; \boldsymbol{Y}_{t-1}, A)$ is

$$p(\boldsymbol{y}_t \mid \boldsymbol{Y}_{t-1}, A) = \int p(\boldsymbol{y}_t \mid \boldsymbol{Y}_{t-1}, \boldsymbol{\theta}_A, A) p(\boldsymbol{\theta}_A \mid \boldsymbol{Y}_{t-1}, A)\, \mathrm{d}\boldsymbol{\theta}_A, \quad (5.1)$$

where $p(\boldsymbol{\theta}_A \mid \boldsymbol{Y}_{t-1}, A)$ is the posterior density

$$p(\boldsymbol{\theta}_A \mid \boldsymbol{Y}_{t-1}, A) \propto p(\boldsymbol{\theta}_A \mid A) \prod_{s=1}^{t-1} p(\boldsymbol{y}_s \mid \boldsymbol{Y}_{s-1}, \boldsymbol{\theta}_A, A)$$

and $p(\boldsymbol{\theta}_A \mid A)$ is the prior density for $\boldsymbol{\theta}_A$. A non-Bayesian approach might construct the parameter estimates $\hat{\boldsymbol{\theta}}_A^{t-1} = f_{t-1}(\boldsymbol{Y}_{t-1})$ and then

$$p(\boldsymbol{y}_t; \boldsymbol{Y}_{t-1}, A) = p(\boldsymbol{y}_t \mid \boldsymbol{Y}_{t-1}, \hat{\boldsymbol{\theta}}_A^{t-1}, A). \quad (5.2)$$

The specific construction of $p(\boldsymbol{y}_t; \boldsymbol{Y}_{t-1}, A)$ is unimportant in this chapter: in the extreme, it could be entirely judgmental. What is critical is that it relies only on information available at time $t - 1$ and that it provides a mathematically complete predictive density for $\boldsymbol{y}_t$. The primitives are these predictive densities and the realizations of the time series $\boldsymbol{y}_t$, denoted $\boldsymbol{y}_t^o$ ("o" for "observed") in situations where the distinction between the random vector and its realization is important. This set of primitives is the one typically used in the few studies that have addressed these questions (see, for example, Diebold et al. 1998, p. 879). As Gneiting et al. (2007, p. 244) notes, the assessment of a predictive distribution on the basis of only $p(\boldsymbol{y}_t; \boldsymbol{Y}_{t-1}, A)$ and $\boldsymbol{y}_t^o$ is consistent with the prequential principle of Dawid (1984).

5.1.1 Log Scoring

The assessment of models and combinations of models considered in this chapter relies on the log predictive score function. For a sample $\boldsymbol{Y}_T = \boldsymbol{Y}_T^o$, the log predictive score function of a single prediction model A is

$$\mathrm{LS}(\boldsymbol{Y}_T^o, A) = \sum_{t=1}^{T} \log p(\boldsymbol{y}_t^o; \boldsymbol{Y}_{t-1}^o, A). \tag{5.3}$$

In a full Bayesian approach,

$$p(\boldsymbol{y}_t; \boldsymbol{Y}_{t-1}, A) = p(\boldsymbol{y}_t \mid \boldsymbol{Y}_{t-1}, A)$$

and (5.3) becomes

$$\begin{aligned}\mathrm{LS}(\boldsymbol{Y}_T^o, A) &= \sum_{t=1}^{T} \log p(\boldsymbol{y}_t^o \mid \boldsymbol{Y}_{t-1}^o, A) = \log p(\boldsymbol{Y}_T^o \mid A) \\ &= \log \int p(\boldsymbol{Y}_T^o, \boldsymbol{\theta}_A \mid A)\, \mathrm{d}\boldsymbol{\theta}_A.\end{aligned}$$

In a parametric non-Bayesian approach (5.2) the log predictive score is

$$\mathrm{LS}(\boldsymbol{Y}_T^o, A) = \sum_{t=1}^{T} \log p(\boldsymbol{y}_t^o \mid \boldsymbol{Y}_{t-1}^o, \hat{\boldsymbol{\theta}}_A^{t-1}, A),$$

which is smaller than the full-sample log-likelihood function evaluated at the maximum-likelihood estimate $\hat{\boldsymbol{\theta}}_A^T$.

Some of the analytical results that follow require that there is a data-generating process D giving rise to the ergodic vector time series $\{\boldsymbol{y}_t\}$. That is, there is a true model D but it is not necessarily one of the models under consideration. For most D and A,

$$\begin{aligned}\mathrm{E}_D&[\mathrm{LS}(\boldsymbol{Y}_T, A)]\\ &= \int \Bigg[\sum_{t=1}^{T} \log p(\boldsymbol{y}_t; \boldsymbol{Y}_{t-1}, A)\Bigg] p(\boldsymbol{Y}_T \mid D)\,\mathrm{d}\boldsymbol{Y}_T\end{aligned}$$

exists and is finite. Given the ergodicity of $\{\boldsymbol{y}_t\}$,

$$\begin{aligned} T^{-1}\mathrm{LS}(\boldsymbol{Y}_T, A) &\xrightarrow{\text{a.s.}} \lim_{T\to\infty} T^{-1}\mathrm{E}_D[\mathrm{LS}(\boldsymbol{Y}_T, A)] \\ &= \mathrm{LS}^*(A; D). \end{aligned} \tag{5.4}$$

Whenever it is necessary to assume a true model D, that will mean that (5.4) is true for D and any model A under consideration.

The log predictive score function is a measure of the out-of-sample prediction track record of the model. Other such scoring rules are, of course, possible: mean square prediction error is perhaps the most familiar. One could imagine using a scoring rule to evaluate the predictive densities provided by a modeler. Suppose that the modeler then produced predictive densities in such a way as to maximize the expected value of the scoring rule, the expectations being taken with respect to the modeler's subjective probability distribution. The scoring rule is said to be proper if, in such a situation, the modeler is led to report a predictive density that is coherent and consistent with his subjective probabilities. (The term "proper" was coined by Winkler and Murphy (1968), but the general idea dates back at least to Brier (1950) and Good (1952).) If the scoring rule depends on $\boldsymbol{Y}_T^o$ and $p(\boldsymbol{y}_t; \boldsymbol{Y}_{t-1}, A)$ only through $p(\boldsymbol{y}_t^o; \boldsymbol{Y}_{t-1}^o, A)$, then it is said to be local (Bernardo 1979).

Any other proper local scoring rule must take the form

$$g(\boldsymbol{Y}_{t-1}^o) + c \sum_{t=1}^{T} \log p(\boldsymbol{y}_t^o; \boldsymbol{Y}_{t-1}^o, A)$$

with $c > 0$, a linear transformation of (5.3). This was shown by de Finetti and Savage (1963) and Shuford et al. (1966) for the case in which the support of $\{\boldsymbol{y}_t\}$ is a finite set of at least three discrete points (for further discussion see Winkler (1969, p. 1,075)). It was subsequently shown for the case of continuously distributed $\{\boldsymbol{y}_t\}$ by Bernardo (1979) (for further discussion see Gneiting and Raftery (2007, p. 366)).

This chapter considers alternative prediction models $A_1, \ldots, A_n$. Propriety of the scoring rule is important in this context because it guarantees that if one of these models were to coincide with the true data-generating process D, then that model would attain the maximum score as $T \to \infty$.

There is a substantial literature on scoring rules for discrete outcomes and in particular for Bernoulli random variables (DeGroot and Fienberg 1982; Clemen et al. 1995). However, as noted in the recent review article by Gneiting et al. (2007, p. 364) and in Bremmes

(2004), the literature on scoring rules for probabilistic forecasts of continuous variables is sparse.

5.1.2 Linear Pooling

This chapter explores some consequences of using the log scoring rule (5.3) to evaluate combinations of probability densities $p(y_t \mid Y^o_{t-1}, A_j)$ $(j = 1, \dots, n)$. There are, of course, many ways in which these densities could be combined, or aggregated; see Genest et al. (1984) for a review and axiomatic approach. McConway (1981) showed that, under mild regularity conditions, if the process of combination is to commute with any possible marginalization of the distributions involved, then the combination must be linear. Moreover, such combinations are trivial to compute, both absolutely and in comparison with alternatives. Hence consider predictive densities of the form

$$\sum_{i=1}^{n} w_i p(y_t; Y^o_{t-1}, A_i), \tag{5.5}$$

where

$$\sum_{i=1}^{n} w_i = 1; \quad w_i \geqslant 0 \quad (i = 1, \dots, n).$$

The restrictions on the weights w_i are necessary and sufficient to ensure that (5.5) is a density function for all values of the weights and for all arguments of the density functions. Evaluate these densities using the log predictive score function

$$\sum_{t=1}^{T} \log\left[\sum_{i=1}^{n} w_i p(y^o_t; Y^o_{t-1}, A_i)\right]. \tag{5.6}$$

Stone (1961) coined the term opinion pool to describe a combination of subjective probability distributions. Linear combinations of these distributions are known as linear opinion pools (Bacharach 1974). The term "prediction pools" describes the setting specific to this chapter. While all models are based on opinions, only formal statistical models are capable of producing the complete predictive densities that, together with the data, constitute the primitives of the prediction pool. The appropriate choice of weights in (5.5) is widely regarded as a difficult and important question. This chapter uses the past performance of the pool to select the weights; in the language of Jacobs (1995), the past constitutes the training sample for the present. Sections 5.3 and 5.5 show that this is easy to do. This chapter compares linear prediction pools using the log scoring rule. An optimal prediction pool is one with weights chosen so as to maximize (5.6).

Hall and Mitchell (2007) proposes combining predictive probability densities by finding the nonnegative weights w_i that maximize (5.6). The motivation for that proposal is asymptotic: as $T \to \infty$, the weights so chosen are those that minimize the Kullback–Leibler directed distance from an assumed data-generating process D to the model (5.5). Hall and Mitchell (2007) shows that direct maximization of (5.6) is more reliable than some other methods, involving probability integral transforms, that have been proposed in the literature. The focus of this chapter is complementary and more analytical, and the examples that follow provide a larger-scale implementation of optimal pooling than does Hall and Mitchell (2007).

The characteristics of optimal prediction pools turn out to be strikingly different from those that are constructed by means of Bayesian model averaging (described in section 2.2) as well as those that result from conventional frequentist testing (which is often problematic since the models are typically nonnested). Given a data-generating process D that produces ergodic $\{y_t\}$, a limiting optimal prediction pool exists, and unless one of the models A_j coincides with D, several of the weights in this pool are typically positive. In contrast, the posterior probability of the model A_j with the smallest Kullback-Leibler directed distance from D will tend to one and all others will tend to zero. Any frequentist procedure based on testing will have a similar property, but with a distance measure specific to the test.

The contrast is rooted in the fact that for both Bayesian model averaging and frequentist tests, the model space is taken to be complete: that is, $A_j = D$ for some j. For optimal prediction pools, the model space is incomplete: that is, it is not assumed that $A_j = D$ for some j, and in general $A_j \neq D$ $(j = 1, \dots, n)$. Section 5.6 shows, by construction, that there exists a model with a log score exceeding that of the optimally scored prediction pool. It follows from proposition 5.2 that $A_j \neq D$ $(j = 1, \dots, n)$.

This chapter develops the basic ideas for a pool of two models (section 5.2) and then applies them to prediction model pools for daily S&P 500 returns for 1972–2005 (section 5.3). It then turns to the general case of pools of n models and studies how changes in the composition of the pool change the optimal weights (section 5.4). Section 5.5 constructs an optimal pool of six alternative prediction models for the S&P 500 returns. Section 5.6 studies the implications of optimal prediction pools for the existence of predictions models, as yet undiscovered, that will compare favorably with those in the pool as assessed by a log predictive scoring rule. The final section concludes.

5.2 Pools of Two Models

Consider the case of two competing prediction models $A_1 \neq A_2$. From (5.4),

$$T^{-1}[\mathrm{LS}(\boldsymbol{Y}_T, A_1) - \mathrm{LS}(\boldsymbol{Y}_T, A_2)] \xrightarrow{\text{a.s.}} \mathrm{LS}^*(A_1; D) - \mathrm{LS}^*(A_2; D).$$

If A_1 corresponds to the data-generating process D, then in general

$$\mathrm{LS}^*(A_1; D) - \mathrm{LS}^*(A_2; D) = \mathrm{LS}^*(D; D) - \mathrm{LS}^*(A_2; D) \geqslant 0$$

and the limiting value coincides with the Kullback-Leibler distance from D to A_2. If in addition A_1 is nested in A_2, then $\mathrm{LS}^*(A_1; D) - \mathrm{LS}^*(A_2; D) = 0$, but in most cases of interest $\mathrm{LS}^*(A_1; D) \neq \mathrm{LS}^*(A_2; D)$ and so if $A_1 = D$ then $\mathrm{LS}^*(A_1; D) - \mathrm{LS}^*(A_2; D) > 0$. These special cases are interesting and informative, but in application most econometricians would agree with the dictum of Box (1980) that all models are false. Indeed, the more illuminating special case might be $\mathrm{LS}^*(A_1; D) - \mathrm{LS}^*(A_2; D) = 0$ when neither model A_j is nested in the other: then both A_1 and A_2 must be false.

In general, $\mathrm{LS}^*(A_1; D) - \mathrm{LS}^*(A_2; D) \neq 0$. For most prediction models constructed from parametric models of the time series $\{\boldsymbol{y}_t\}$, a closely related implication is that one of the two models will almost surely be rejected in favor of the other as $T \to \infty$. For example, in the Bayesian approach (5.1) the Bayes factor in favor of one model over the other will converge to zero, and in the non-Bayesian construction (5.2) the likelihood ratio test or another test appropriate to the estimates $\hat{\boldsymbol{\theta}}^t_{A_j}$ will reject one model in favor of the other.

Given the two prediction models A_1 and A_2, the prediction pool $A = \{A_1, A_2\}$ consists of all prediction models

$$p(\boldsymbol{y}_t; \boldsymbol{Y}_{t-1}, A) = wp(\boldsymbol{y}_t; \boldsymbol{Y}_{t-1}, A_1) + (1-w)p(\boldsymbol{y}_t; \boldsymbol{Y}_{t-1}, A_2), \quad (5.7)$$

where $w \in [0, 1]$. The corresponding log predictive score function is

$$f_T(w) = \sum_{t=1}^{T} \log[wp(\boldsymbol{y}^o_t; \boldsymbol{Y}^o_{t-1}, A_1) + (1-w)p(\boldsymbol{y}^o_t; \boldsymbol{Y}^o_{t-1}, A_2)]. \quad (5.8)$$

The optimal prediction pool corresponds to $w^*_T = \text{argmax}_w\, f_T(w)$ in (5.8).[1] At time $t-1$ the determination of such a pool was impossible for the purposes of forming the elements $wp(\boldsymbol{y}_t; \boldsymbol{Y}^o_{t-1}, A_1) + (1-w)p(\boldsymbol{y}_t; \boldsymbol{Y}^o_{t-1}, A_2)$ $(t = 1, \dots, T)$ because it is based on the entire sample. However, the weights w could be determined recursively at each date t based on information through $t-1$. It will subsequently be seen that the

[1] The setup in (5.8) is formally similar to the nesting proposed by Quandt (1974) in order to test the null hypothesis $A_1 = D$ against the alternative $A_2 = D$ (see also Gourieroux and Monfort (1989, section 22.2.7)). That is not the objective here. Moreover, Quandt's test involves simultaneously maximizing the function in the parameters of both models and w, and is therefore equivalent to the attempt to estimate by maximum likelihood the mixture models discussed in section 5.6; Quandt (1974) clearly recognizes the pitfalls associated with this procedure.

required computations are practical, and in the examples in the next section there is almost no difference between the optimal pool considered here and those created recursively when the alternative procedures are evaluated using a log scoring rule.

The first derivative of f_T, denoted $f_T'(w)$, is

$$\sum_{t=1}^{T} \frac{p(y_t^o; Y_{t-1}^o, A_1) - p(y_t^o; Y_{t-1}^o, A_2)}{wp(y_t^o; Y_{t-1}^o, A_1) + (1-w)p(y_t^o; Y_{t-1}^o, A_2)}. \quad (5.9)$$

The second derivative of f_T, denoted $f_T''(w)$, is

$$-\sum_{t=1}^{T} \left[\frac{p(y_t^o; Y_{t-1}^o, A_1) - p(y_t^o; Y_{t-1}^o, A_2)}{wp(y_t^o; Y_{t-1}^o, A_1) + (1-w)p(y_t^o; Y_{t-1}^o, A_2)} \right]^2.$$

Notice that $f_T''(w) \leqslant 0$; and pathological cases aside, $f_T''(w) < 0$. For all $w \in [0,1]$, $T^{-1} f_T(w) \xrightarrow{\text{a.s.}} f(w)$. If

$$\lim_{T\to\infty} T^{-1} \sum_{t=1}^{T} \mathrm{E}_D |p(y_t; Y_{t-1}, A_1) - p(y_t; Y_{t-1}, A_2)| \neq 0, \quad (5.10)$$

then $f(w)$ is concave. The condition (5.10) does not necessarily hold, but the only common case in which it does not seems to be when one of the models nests the other and the restrictions that create the nesting are correct for the pseudotrue parameter vector. The focus here is on prediction models A_1 and A_2 that are typically nonnested and, in fact, have predictive densities with substantially different functional forms. Henceforth it will be assumed that (5.10) is true. Given this assumption, $w_T^* = \operatorname{argmax}_w f_T(w)$ converges almost surely to the unique value $w^* = \operatorname{argmax}_w f(w)$. Thus for a given data-generating process D there is a unique limiting optimal prediction pool. As shown in Hall and Mitchell (2007) this prediction pool minimizes the Kullback–Leibler directed distance from D to the prediction model (5.5).

It will prove useful to distinguish between several kinds of prediction pools, based on the properties of f_T. If $w_T^* \in (0,1)$, then A_1 and A_2 are each *competitive* in the pool $\{A_1, A_2\}$. If $w_T^* = 1$, then A_1 is *dominant* in the pool $\{A_1, A_2\}$ and A_2 is *excluded* in that pool;[2] equivalently, $f_T'(1) \geqslant 0$, which amounts to

$$T^{-1} \sum_{t=1}^{T} \frac{p(y_t^o; Y_{t-1}^o, A_2)}{p(y_t^o; Y_{t-1}^o, A_1)} \leqslant 1.$$

By mild extension, A_1 and A_2 are each competitive in the population pool $\{A_1, A_2\}$ if $w^* \in (0,1)$, and if $w^* = 1$ then A_1 is dominant in the population pool and A_2 is excluded in that pool.

Some special cases are interesting not because they are likely to occur but because they help to illuminate the relationship between prediction pools and concepts familiar from model comparison. First consider the hypothetical case $A_1 = D$.

Proposition 5.1. *If $A_1 = D$, then A_1 is dominant in the population pool $\{A_1, A_2\}$ and $f'(1) = 0$.*

Proof. If $A_1 = D$,

$$f'(1) = \lim_{T\to\infty} T^{-1} \sum_{t=1}^{T} \mathrm{E}_D\left[1 - \frac{p(y_t; Y_{t-1}, A_2)}{p(y_t; Y_{t-1}, D)}\right] = 0.$$

From (5.9) and the strict concavity of f it follows that A_1 is dominant in the population pool. □

[2] Dominance is a necessary condition for forecast encompassing (Chong and Hendry 1986) asymptotically, but it is weaker than forecast encompassing.

A second illuminating hypothetical case is

$$\mathrm{LS}^*(A_1;D) = \mathrm{LS}^*(A_2;D).$$

Given (5.10), then $A_1 \neq D$ and $A_2 \neq D$ in view of proposition 5.1. The implication of this result for practical work is that if two nonnested models have roughly the same log score, then neither is "true." Section 5.6 returns to this implication at greater length.

Turning to the more realistic case $\mathrm{LS}^*(A_1;D) \neq \mathrm{LS}^*(A_2;D)$, $w^* \in (0,1)$ also implies that $A_1 \neq D$ and that $A_2 \neq D$. In fact, one never observes f, of course, but the familiar log scale of $f_T(w)$ provides some indication of the strength of the evidence against the proposition that $A_1 = D$ or $A_2 = D$. There is a literature on testing that formalizes this idea in the context of (5.7) (see Gourieroux and Monfort 1989, chapter 22; Quandt 1974). The motivation is not to demonstrate that any prediction model is false: it is known at the outset that this is the case. What is more important is that (5.7) evaluated at w_T^* provides a lower bound on the improvement in the log score predictive density that could be attained by models not in the pool, including models not yet discovered. Section 5.6 returns to this point.

If $w^* \in (0,1)$ then, for a sufficiently large sample size, the optimal pool will have a log predictive score superior to that of either A_1 or A_2 alone, and as sample size increases, $w_T^* \xrightarrow{\text{a.s.}} w^*$. This is in marked contrast to conventional Bayesian model combination or non-Bayesian tests. Both will exclude one model or the other asymptotically, although the procedures are formally distinct. For Bayesian model combination the contrast is due to the fact that the conventional setup conditions on one of either $D = A_1$ or $D = A_2$ being true. As has been seen, in this case the posterior probability of A_1 and w_T^* have the same limit. The incompleteness of the model space, that is, $A_1 \neq D$ and $A_2 \neq D$, changes the conventional assumptions. It leads to an entirely different result: even models that are arbitrarily inferior, as measured by Bayes factors, can substantially improve predictions from the superior model as indicated by a log scoring rule. For non-Bayesian testing the explanation is the same: since a true test rejects one model and accepts the other, it also conditions on one of either $D = A_1$ or $D = A_2$ being true.

5.3 Examples of Two-Model Pools

This section illustrates some properties of two-model pools using daily percentage log returns of the S&P 500 index and six alternative models for these returns. All of the models used rolling samples of 1,250 trading days (about five years). The first sample consisted of returns from January 3, 1972, through December 14, 1976, and the first predictive density evaluation was for the return on December 15, 1976. The last predictive density evaluation was for the return on December 16, 2005 ($T = 7{,}324$).

Three of the models are estimated by maximum likelihood and predictive densities are formed by substituting the estimates for the unknown parameters: a Gaussian i.i.d. model ("Gaussian," hereafter); a Gaussian generalized autoregressive conditional heteroscedasticity model with parameters $p = q = 1$, or GARCH$(1, 1)$ ("GARCH"), which is described in section 3.1.3; and a Gaussian exponential GARCH model with $p = q = 1$ ("EGARCH" (Nelson 1991)). Three of the models formed full Bayesian predictive densities

Table 5.1. Log predictive scores of the alternative models.

Gaussian	−10,570.80
GARCH	−9,574.41
EGARCH	−9,549.41
t-GARCH	−9,317.50
SV	−9,460.93
HMNM	−9,336.60

using Markov chain Monte Carlo algorithms: a GARCH model with i.i.d. Student-t shocks ("t-GARCH" (Dueker 1997)); the stochastic volatility model of Jacquier et al. (1994) ("SV"), detailed in section 3.1.4; and the hierarchical Markov normal mixture model with serial correlation and $m_1 = m_2 = 5$ latent states described in Geweke and Amisano (forthcoming) ("HMNM").

Table 5.1 provides the log predictive score for each model. That for t-GARCH exceeds that of the nearest competitor, HMNM, by 19. Results for these two models are based on full Bayesian inference but the log predictive scores are not the same as log marginal likelihoods because the early part of the data set is omitted and because rolling rather than full samples are used. Nevertheless, the difference between these two models strongly suggests that a formal Bayesian model comparison would yield overwhelming posterior odds in favor of t-GARCH. Of course the evidence against the other models in favor of t-GARCH is even stronger: 143 against SV, 232 against EGARCH, 257 against GARCH, and 1,253 against Gaussian.

Pools of two models, one of which is t-GARCH, reveal that t-GARCH is not dominant in all of these pools. Figure 5.1 shows the function $f_T(w)$ for pools of two models, one of which is t-GARCH, with w denoting

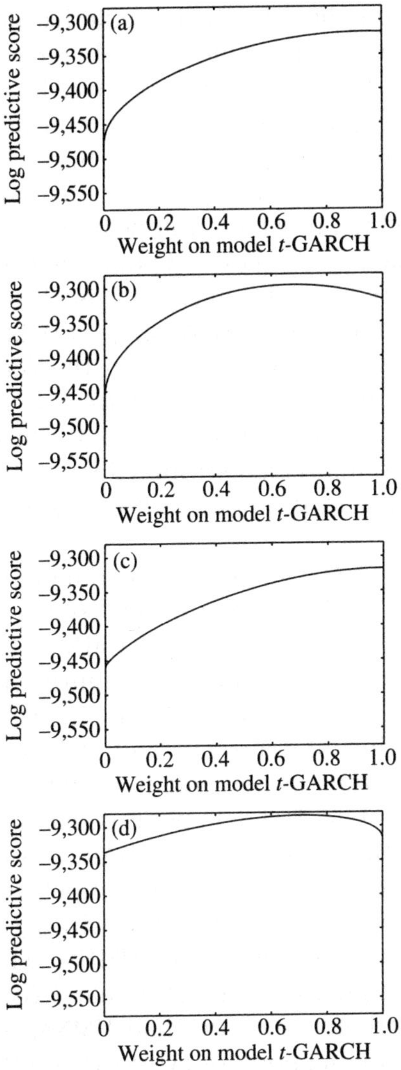

Figure 5.1. Functions $f_T(w)$ in some two-model pools. (a) GARCH, t-GARCH. (b) EGARCH, t-GARCH. (c) SV, t-GARCH. (d) HMNM, t-GARCH.

the weight on the t-GARCH predictive density. The vertical scale is the same in each panel. All functions $f_T(w)$ are, of course, concave. In the GARCH and t-GARCH pool, $f_T(w)$ has an internal maximum at $w = 0.944$ with $f_T(0.944) = -9{,}315.50$, whereas $f_T(1) = -9{,}317.12$. This distinction is barely detectable in panel (a), in which it appears that $f_T'(w) \approxeq 0$. For the EGARCH and t-GARCH pool, and for the HMNM and t-GARCH pool, the maximum is clearly internal. For the SV and t-GARCH pool, $f_T(w)$ is monotone increasing, with $f_T'(1) = 1.96$. In the Gaussian and t-GARCH pool, not shown in figure 5.1, t-GARCH is again dominant, with $f_T'(1) = 54.4$. Thus, while all two-model comparisons strongly favor t-GARCH, it is dominant only in the pool with Gaussian and in the pool with SV.

Figure 5.2 portrays $f_T(w)$ for two-model pools consisting of HMNM and one other predictive density, with w denoting the weight on HMNM. The scale of the vertical axis is the same as in figure 5.1 in all panels except (a), which shows $f_T(w)$ in the two-model pool consisting of Gaussian and HMNM. The latter model nests the former and it is dominant in this pool, with $f_T'(1) = 108.3$. In pools consisting of HMNM on the one hand and GARCH, EGARCH, or SV on the other, the models are mutually competitive. Thus SV is excluded in a two-model pool with t-GARCH, but not in a two-model pool with HMNM. This is not a logical consequence of the fact that t-GARCH has a higher log predictive score than HMNM. Indeed, the optimal two-model pool for EGARCH and HMNM has a higher log predictive score than any two-model pool that includes t-GARCH, as is evident by comparing figure 5.2(c) with all the panels of figure 5.1.

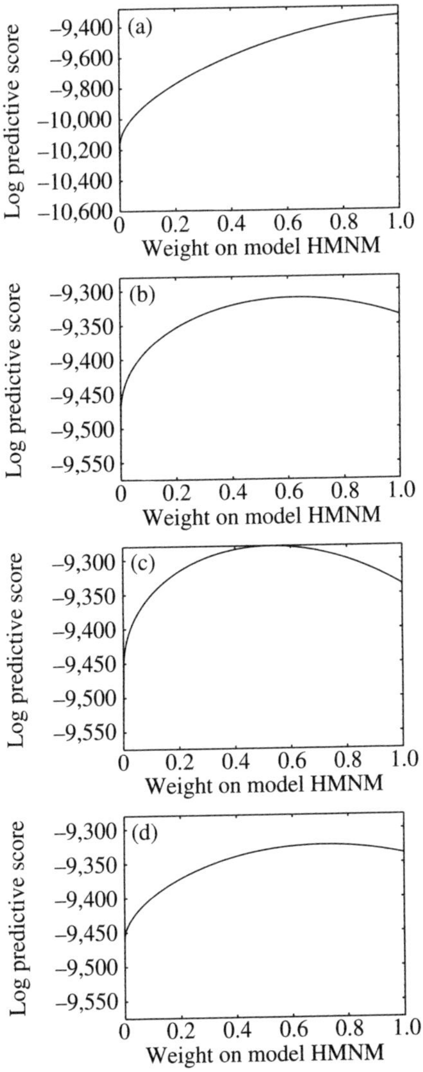

Figure 5.2. Functions $f_T(w)$ in some two-model pools. (a) Gaussian, HMNM. (b) GARCH, HMNM. (c) EGARCH, HMNM. (d) SV, HMNM.

Table 5.2. Optimal pools of two predictive models.

	Gaussian	GARCH	EGARCH	t-GARCH	SV	HMNM
Gaussian	—	−9,539.7 −9,541.4	−9,505.6 −9,507.7	−9,317.5 −9,318.6	−9,460.4 −9,462.0	−9,336.6 −9,337.5
GARCH	0.957 0.943	—	−9,514.3 −9,516.5	−9,317.1 −9,317.5	−9,417.9 −9,419.8	−9,310.6 −9,313.5
EGARCH	0.943 0.920	0.628 0.386	—	−9,296.1 −9,298.3	−9,380.1 −9,383.1	−9,280.3 −9,282.7
t-GARCH	1.000 0.984	0.944 0.931	0.677 0.861	—	−9,317.5 −9,318.1	−9,284.7 −9,287.3
SV	0.986 0.971	0.494 0.384	0.421 0.453	0.000 0.007	—	−9,323.9 −9,325.5
HMNM	1.000 0.996	0.628 0.611	0.529 0.670	0.289 0.307	0.713 0.787	—

Table 5.2 summarizes some key characteristics of all the two-model pools that can be created for these predictive densities. The entries above the main diagonal indicate the log scores of the optimal pools of two prediction models. The entries below the main diagonal indicate the weights w_T^* on the models in the row entries. In each cell there is a pair of entries. The upper entry reflects pool optimization exactly as described in the previous section. In particular, the optimal prediction model weight is determined just once, on the basis of the predictive densities for all T data points. This scheme could not be used in practice because only past data are available for optimization. The lower entry in each pair reflects pool optimization using the predictive densities $p(y_s^o; Y_{s-1}^o, A_j)$ $(s = 1, \dots, t-1)$ to form the optimal pooled predictive density for y_t. The log scores (above the main diagonal in table 5.2) are the sums of the log scores for pools formed in this way. The weights (below the main diagonal in table 5.2) are averages of the weights w_t^* taken across all T predictive densities. (For $t = 1$, w_1^* was arbitrarily set at 0.5.)

For example, in the t-GARCH and HMNM pool, the log score using the optimal weight based on all T observations is −9,284.7. If, instead, the optimal weight is recalculated in each period using only past predictive likelihoods, then the log score is −9,287.3. The weight on the HMNM model is 0.289 in the former case, and the average weight on this model is 0.307 in the latter case. Note that in every case the log score is lower when it is determined using only past predictive likelihoods than it is when it is determined using the entire sample. But the values are, at most, about 3 points lower. The weights themselves show some marked differences; pools involving EGARCH seem to exhibit the largest contrasts. The fact that the two methods can produce substantial differences in weights, while the log scores are always nearly the same, is consistent with the small values of $|f_T''(w)|$ in large neighborhoods of the optimal value of w evident in figures 5.1 and 5.2.

Figure 5.3 shows the evolution of the weight w_t^* in some two-model pools when pools are optimized using only past realizations of predictive densities. Unsurprisingly, w_t^* fluctuates violently at the start of the sample. Although the predictive densities are based on rolling five-year samples, w_t^* should converge almost surely to a limit under the conditions specified in section 5.2. The HMNM and t-GARCH pool (panel (a)) might be interpreted as displaying this convergence, but the case for the EGARCH pools is not so strong.

Whether or not section 5.2 provides a good asymptotic paradigm for the behavior of w_t^* is beside the point, however. The important fact is that a number of pools of two models outperform the model that performs best on its own (t-GARCH), performance being assessed by the log scoring rule in each case. The best of these two-model pools (HMNM and EGARCH) does not even involve t-GARCH, and it outperforms t-GARCH by 37 points. These findings illustrate the fresh perspective brought to model combination by linear pools of prediction models. Extending pools to more than two models provides additional insights.

5.4 Pools of Multiple Models

In a prediction pool with n models the log predictive score function is

$$f_T(\boldsymbol{w}) = \sum_{t=1}^{T} \log\left[\sum_{i=1}^{n} w_i p(\boldsymbol{y}_t; \boldsymbol{Y}_{t-1}, A_i)\right],$$

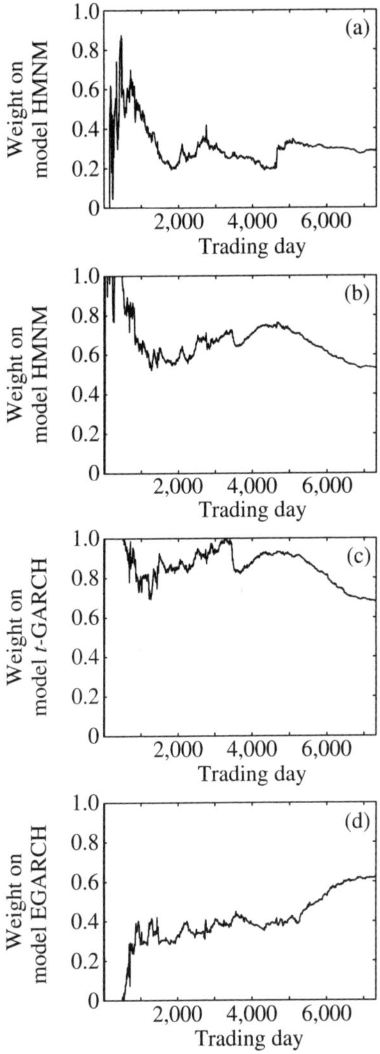

Figure 5.3. Evolution of model weights in some two-model pools. (a) HMNM, t-GARCH. (b) HMNM, EGARCH. (c) t-GARCH, EGARCH. (d) EGARCH, GARCH.

where $\boldsymbol{w} = (w_1, \dots, w_n)'$, $w_i \geqslant 0$ $(i = 1, \dots, n)$, and $\sum_{i=1}^{n} w_i = 1$. Denote by $f(\boldsymbol{w})$ the limit (as $T \to \infty$) of

$$T^{-1} f_T(\boldsymbol{w}) \xrightarrow{\text{a.s.}} \lim_{T\to\infty} T^{-1} \times \int \sum_{t=1}^{T} \log\Bigg[\sum_{i=1}^{n} w_i p(\boldsymbol{y}_t; \boldsymbol{Y}_{t-1}, A_i)\Bigg] p(\boldsymbol{Y}_T \mid D)\, \mathrm{d}\boldsymbol{Y}_T.$$

Given the assumptions about the data-generating process D,

$$T^{-1} f_T(\boldsymbol{w}) \xrightarrow{\text{a.s.}} f(\boldsymbol{w}).$$

Let p_{ti} denote $p(\boldsymbol{y}_t^o; \boldsymbol{Y}_{t-1}^o, A_i)$ $(t = 1, \dots, T;\ i = 1, \dots, n)$. Substituting $1 - \sum_{i=2}^{n} w_i$ for w_1,

$$\frac{\partial f_T(\boldsymbol{w})}{\partial w_i} = \sum_{t=1}^{T} \frac{p_{ti} - p_{t1}}{\sum_{k=1}^{n} w_k p_{tk}} \quad (i = 2, \dots, n) \tag{5.11}$$

and

$$\frac{\partial^2 f_T(\boldsymbol{w})}{\partial w_i \partial w_j} = -\sum_{t=1}^{T} \frac{(p_{ti} - p_{t1})(p_{tj} - p_{t1})}{[\sum_{k=1}^{n} w_k p_{tk}]^2} \quad (i, j = 2, \dots, n).$$

The $(n-1) \times (n-1)$ Hessian matrix $\partial^2 f_T / \partial \boldsymbol{w} \partial \boldsymbol{w}'$ is nonpositive definite for all $\boldsymbol{w}$ and, pathological cases aside, negative definite. Thus $f(\boldsymbol{w})$ is strictly concave on the unit simplex. Given the evaluations p_{ti} over the sample from the alternative prediction models, finding $\boldsymbol{w}_T^* = \operatorname{argmax}_{\boldsymbol{w}} f_T(\boldsymbol{w})$ is a straightforward convex programming problem. The limit $f(\boldsymbol{w})$ is also concave in $\boldsymbol{w}$ and $\boldsymbol{w}_T \xrightarrow{\text{a.s.}} \boldsymbol{w}^* = \operatorname{argmax}_{\boldsymbol{w}} f(\boldsymbol{w})$.

Proposition 5.1 generalizes immediately to pools of multiple models.

Proposition 5.2. *If $A_1 = D$, then A_1 is dominant in the population pool $\{A_1, \dots, A_n\}$ and*

$$\left.\frac{\partial f(\boldsymbol{w})}{\partial w_j}\right|_{\boldsymbol{w}=\tilde{\boldsymbol{w}}} = 0 \quad (j = 1, \dots, n),$$

where $\tilde{\boldsymbol{w}} = (1, 0, \dots, 0)'$.

Proof. From (5.11),

$$\begin{aligned}\left.\frac{\partial f(\boldsymbol{w})}{\partial w_j}\right|_{\boldsymbol{w}=\tilde{\boldsymbol{w}}} &= \lim_{T\to\infty} T^{-1} \sum_{t=1}^{T} \mathrm{E}_D\left[\frac{p(\boldsymbol{y}_t; \boldsymbol{Y}_{t-1}, A_j)}{p(\boldsymbol{y}_t; \boldsymbol{Y}_{t-1}, D)} - 1\right] \\ &= 0 \quad (j = 2, \dots, n),\end{aligned}$$

and consequently

$$\left.\frac{\partial f(\boldsymbol{w})}{\partial w_1}\right|_{\boldsymbol{w}=\tilde{\boldsymbol{w}}} = 0$$

as well. From the concavity of $f(\boldsymbol{w})$, $\boldsymbol{w}^* = \tilde{\boldsymbol{w}}$. □

Extending the definitions of section 5.2, models $A_1, \dots, A_m$ ($m < n$) are *jointly excluded* in the pool $\{A_1, \dots, A_n\}$ if $\sum_{i=1}^{m} w_{Ti}^* = 0$; they are *jointly competitive* in the pool if $0 < \sum_{i=1}^{m} w_{Ti}^* < 1$; and they *jointly dominate* the pool if $\sum_{i=1}^{m} w_{Ti}^* = 1$. Obviously, any pool has a smallest dominant subset. A pool trivially dominates itself. There are relations between exclusion, competitiveness, and dominance that are useful in interpreting and constructing optimal prediction pools.

Proposition 5.3. *If $\{A_1, \dots, A_m\}$ dominates the pool $\{A_1, \dots, A_n\}$, then $\{A_1, \dots, A_m\}$ dominates*

$$\{A_1, \dots, A_m, A_{j_1}, \dots, A_{j_k}\}$$

for all $\{j_1, \dots, j_k\} \subseteq \{m+1, \dots, n\}$.

Proof. By assumption, $\{A_{m+1}, \ldots, A_n\}$ is excluded in the pool $\{A_1, \ldots, A_n\}$. The pool

$$\{A_1, \ldots, A_m, A_{j_1}, \ldots, A_{j_k}\}$$

imposes the constraints $w_i = 0$ for all $i > m$, $i \neq \{j_1, \ldots, j_k\}$. Since $\{A_{m+1}, \ldots, A_n\}$ was excluded in $\{A_1, \ldots, A_n\}$, these constraints are not binding. Therefore $\{A_{j_1}, \ldots, A_{j_k}\}$ is excluded in the pool $\{A_1, \ldots, A_m, A_{j_1}, \ldots, A_{j_k}\}$. □

Thus a dominant subset of a pool is dominant in all subsets of the pool in which it is included.

Proposition 5.4. *If* $\{A_1, \ldots, A_m\}$ *dominates all pools*

$$\{A_1, \ldots, A_m, A_j\} \quad (j = m + 1, \ldots, n),$$

then $\{A_1, \ldots, A_m\}$ *dominates the pool* $\{A_1, \ldots, A_n\}$.

Proof. The result is a consequence of the concavity of the objective functions. The assumption implies that there exist optimal weights $w_2^*, \ldots, w_m^*$ such that

$$\partial f_T(w_2^*, \ldots, w_m^*, w_j)/\partial w_j < 0$$

when evaluated at $w_j = 0$ $(j = m + 1, \ldots, n)$. Taken jointly these $n - m$ conditions are necessary and sufficient for $w_{m+1} = \cdots = w_n = 0$ in the optimal pool created from the models $\{A_{1,}, \ldots, A_n\}$. □

The converse of proposition 5.4 is a special case of proposition 5.3. Taken together these propositions provide an efficient means of showing that a small group of models is dominant in a large pool.

Proposition 5.5. *The set of models* $\{A_1, \ldots, A_m\}$ *is excluded in the pool* $\{A_1, \ldots, A_n\}$ *if and only if* A_j *is excluded in each of the pools* $\{A_j, A_{m+1}, \ldots, A_n\}$ $(j = 1, \ldots, m)$.

Proof. This is an immediate consequence of the first-order conditions for exclusion, just as in the proof of proposition 5.4. □

Proposition 5.6. *If the model A_1 is excluded in all pools (A_1, A_i) $(i = 2, \dots, n)$, then A_1 is excluded in the pool $(A_1, \dots, A_n)$.*

Proof. From (5.9) and the concavity of f_T the assumption implies that

$$T^{-1} \sum_{t=1}^{T} \frac{p_{t1}}{p_{ti}} \leqslant 1 \quad (i = 2, \dots, n). \tag{5.12}$$

Let $\tilde{w}_i$ $(i = 2, \dots, n)$ be the optimal weights in the pool $(A_2, \dots, A_n)$. From (5.11),

$$T^{-1} \sum_{t=1}^{T} \frac{p_{ti}}{\sum_{j=2}^{n} \tilde{w}_j p_{tj}} = \lambda \quad \text{if } \tilde{w}_i > 0 \ (i = 2, \dots, n) \tag{5.13}$$

for some positive but unspecified constant λ. From Jensen's inequality and (5.12),

$$T^{-1} \sum_{t=1}^{T} \frac{p_{t1}}{\sum_{j=2}^{n} \tilde{w}_j p_{tj}} < T^{-1} \sum_{t=1}^{T} \sum_{i=2}^{n} \tilde{w}_i \frac{p_{t1}}{p_{ti}} < 1. \tag{5.14}$$

Suppose that $\tilde{w}_i > 0$. From (5.13),

$$\begin{aligned} T^{-1} \sum_{t=1}^{T} \frac{p_{ti}}{\sum_{j=2}^{n} \tilde{w}_j p_{tj}} &= T^{-1} \sum_{T=1}^{T} \sum_{\ell=2}^{n} \tilde{w}_\ell \frac{p_{t\ell}}{\sum_{j=2}^{n} \tilde{w}_j p_{tj}} \\ &= 1 \quad (i = 2, \dots, n). \end{aligned} \tag{5.15}$$

From (5.14) and (5.15),

$$T^{-1} \sum_{t=1}^{T} \frac{p_{ti} - p_{t1}}{\sum_{j=2}^{n} \tilde{w}_j p_{tj}} \geqslant 0 \quad (i = 2, \dots, n).$$

Since $w_1 = 1 - \sum_{i=2}^{n} w_i$, it follows from (5.11) that $\partial f_T(\boldsymbol{w})/\partial w_1 \leqslant 0$ at the point $\boldsymbol{w} = (0, \tilde{w}_2, \dots, \tilde{w}_n)'$. Because f_T is concave this is necessary and sufficient for A_1 to be excluded in the pool $(A_1, \dots, A_n)$. □

Proposition 5.6 shows that one can establish the exclusion of A_1 in the pool $\{A_1, \dots, A_n\}$, or for that matter any subset of the pool $\{A_1, \dots, A_n\}$ that includes A_1, by showing that A_1 is excluded in the two-model pools $\{A_1, A_i\}$ for all A_i that make up the larger pool.

The converse of proposition 5.6 is false. That is, a model can be excluded in a pool with three or more models and yet be competitive in some (or even all) pairwise pools. Consider $T = 2$ and the following values of p_{ti}:

	A_1	A_2	A_3
$t = 1$	0.4	0.1	1.0
$t = 2$	0.4	1.0	0.1

The model A_1 is competitive in the pools $\{A_1, A_2\}$ and $\{A_1, A_3\}$ because in (5.9) $f_T'(0) > 0$ and $f_T'(1) < 0$ in each pool. In the optimal pool $\{A_2, A_3\}$ the models A_2 and A_3 have equal weight with

$$\sum_{t=1}^{2} \sum_{j=2}^{3} \tilde{w}_j p_{tj} = 0.55.$$

The first-order conditions in (5.11) are

$$\frac{\partial f_T(\boldsymbol{w})}{\partial w_2} = \frac{\partial f_T(\boldsymbol{w})}{\partial w_3} = \frac{0.3}{0.55} > 0,$$

and therefore the constraint $w_1 \geqslant 0$ is binding in the optimal pool $\{A_1, A_2, A_3\}$. The contours of the log predictive score function are shown in figure 5.4(a).

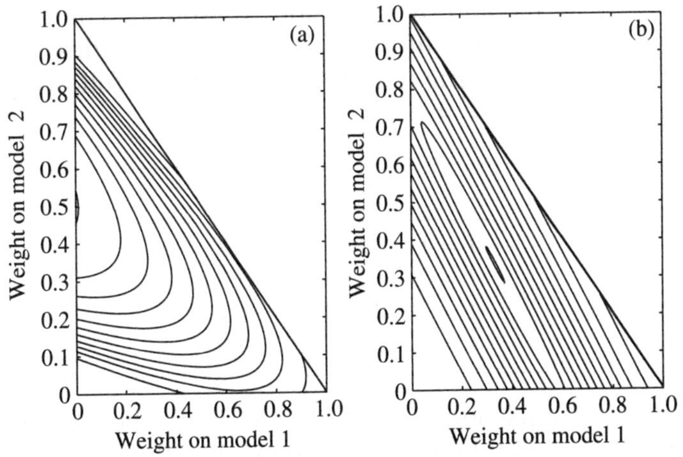

Figure 5.4. Counterexamples relevant to proposition 5.6.

Notice also in this example that

$$\begin{aligned} \mathrm{LS}(\boldsymbol{Y}_T^o, A_1) &= -1.833 > -2.302 \\ &= \mathrm{LS}(\boldsymbol{Y}_T^o, A_2) = \mathrm{LS}(\boldsymbol{Y}_T^o, A_3), \end{aligned}$$

and thus the model with the highest log score can be excluded from the optimal pool. The same result holds in the population: the Kullback–Leibler distance from D to A_1 may be less than the distance from D to A_j $(j = 2, \dots, n)$ and yet A_1 may be excluded in the population pool $\{A_1, \dots, A_n\}$ so long as $n > 2$. If $n = 2$ then the model with the higher log score is always included in the optimal pool.

No significantly stronger version of proposition 5.6 appears to be true. Consider the conjecture that if model A_1 is excluded in one of the pools $\{A_1, A_i\}$ $(i = 2, \dots, n)$, then A_1 is excluded in the pool $\{A_1, \dots, A_n\}$. The contrapositive of this claim is that if A_1 is competitive in $\{A_1, \dots, A_n\}$, then it is competitive in $\{A_1, A_i\}$

$(i = 2, \ldots, n)$, and by extension A_1 wold be competitive in any subset of $\{A_1, \ldots, A_n\}$ that includes A_1. That this is not true may be seen from the following example with $T = 4$:

	A_1	A_2	A_3
$t = 1$	0.8	0.9	1.3
$t = 2$	1.2	1.1	0.7
$t = 3$	0.9	1.0	1.1
$t = 4$	1.1	1.0	0.9

The optimal pool $\{A_1, A_2, A_3\}$ weights the models equally, as may be verified from (5.11). But A_1 is excluded in the pool $\{A_1, A_2\}$: assigning w to A_1, (5.9) shows that

$$f_T'(0) = \frac{-0.1}{0.9} + \frac{0.1}{1.1} + \frac{-0.1}{1} + \frac{0.1}{1} < 0.$$

The contours of the log predictive score function are shown in figure 5.4(b).

5.5 Multiple-Model Pools: An Example

Using the same S&P 500 returns data set described in section 5.3 it is easy to find the optimal pool of all six prediction models described in that section. (The optimization required 0.22 seconds using conventional Matlab software, illustrating the trivial computations required for log score optimal pooling once the predictive density evaluations are available.) The first line of table 5.3 indicates the composition of the optimal pool and the associated log score. The EGARCH, t-GARCH, and HMNM models are jointly dominant in this pool

Table 5.3. Optimal pools of 6 and 5 models.

Gaussian	GARCH	EGARCH	*t*-GARCH	SV	HMNM	Log score
0.000	0.000	0.319	0.417	0.000	0.264	−9,264.83
0.000	0.060	—	0.653	0.000	0.286	−9,284.30
0.000	0.000	0.471	—	0.000	0.529	−9,280.34
0.000	0.000	0.323	0.677	0.000	—	−9,296.08

while the Gaussian, GARCH, and SVOL models are excluded. In the optimal pool the highest weight is given to *t*-GARCH, the next highest to EGARCH, and the smallest positive weight to HMNM.

Weights do not indicate a predictive model's contribution to the log score, however. The next three lines of table 5.3 show the impact of excluding one of the models dominant in the optimal pool. The results show that HMNM makes the largest contribution to the optimal score, 31.25 points; EGARCH the next largest, 19.47 points; and *t*-GARCH the smallest, 15.51 points. This ranking strictly reverses the ranking by weight in the optimal pool. When EGARCH is removed GARCH enters the dominant pool with a small weight, whereas the same models are excluded in the optimal pool when either *t*-GARCH or HMNM is removed.

These characteristics of the pool are evident in figure 5.5, which shows log predictive score contours for the dominant three-model pool on the unit simplex. Weights for EGARCH and *t*-GARCH are shown explicitly on the horizontal and vertical axes, with residual weight on HMNM. Thus the origin corresponds to HMNM, the lower right vertex of the simplex to EGARCH, and the upper left vertex to *t*-GARCH. Values of the log score for the pool at those points can be read from table 5.1. The small circles indicate optimal pools

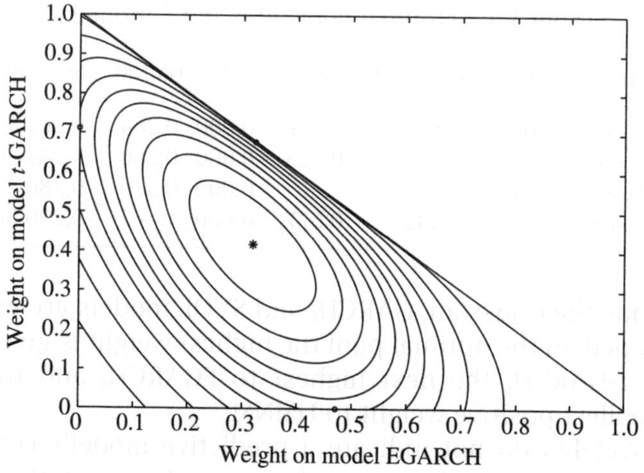

Figure 5.5. The log score function for the prediction pool consisting of the three jointly dominant models.

formed from two of the three models: EGARCH and HMNM on the horizontal axis, *t*-GARCH and HMNM on the vertical axis, and EGARCH and *t*-GARCH on the diagonal. Values of the log score for the pool at those points can be read from the last three entries in the last column of table 5.3. The optimal pool is indicated by the asterisk. Moving away from this point, the log score function is much steeper moving toward the diagonal than toward either axis. This reflects the large contribution of HMNM to the log score relative to the other two models just noted.

The optimal pool could not be used in actual predictions during the years 1975 through 2005 because the weights draw on all of the returns from that period. As in section 5.3, optimal weights can be computed each day to form a prediction pool for the next day. These weights are portrayed in figure 5.6. There is substantial movement in the weights, with

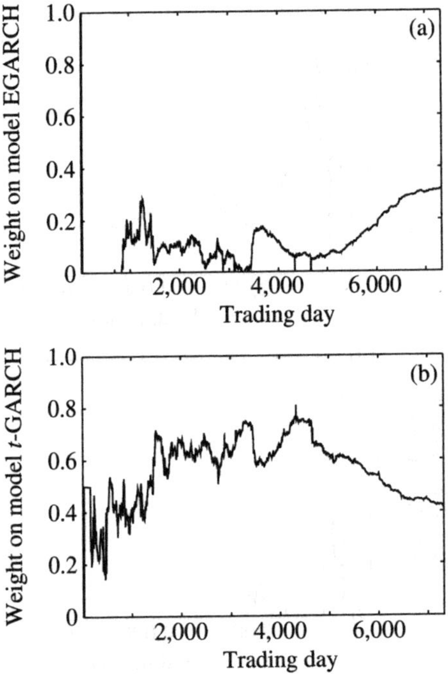

Figure 5.6. Evolution of model weights in the six-model pool. (a) Weight on model EGARCH. (b) Weight on model t-GARCH.

a noted tendency for the weight on EGARCH to be increasing at the expense of t-GARCH, even late in the period. Nevertheless, the log score function for the prediction model pool constructed in this way is $-9{,}267.82$, just 3 points lower than the pool optimized over the entire sample. Moreover, this value substantially exceeds the log score for any model over the same period, or for any optimal pool of two models (see table 5.3).

This insensitivity of the pool log score to substantial changes in the weights reflects the shallowness

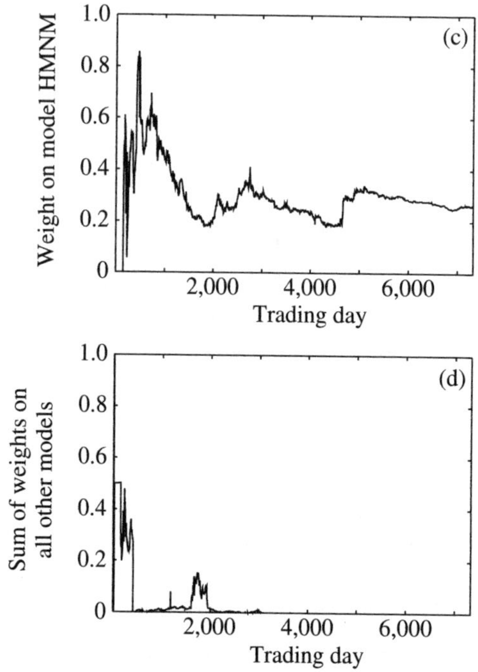

Figure 5.6. (*Continued.*) (c) Weight on model HMNM. (d) Sum of weights on all other models.

of the objective function near its mode: a pool with equal weights for the three dominant models has a log score of −9,265.62, almost as high as that of the optimal pool. This leaves essentially no possible return (as measured by the log score) to more elaborate methods of combining models like bagging (Breiman 1996) or boosting (Friedman et al. 2000). Whether these circumstances are typical can be established in future research by applying the same kind of analysis undertaken in this section for the relevant data and models.

5.6 Pooling and Model Improvement

The linear pool $\{A_1, A_2\}$ is superficially similar to the mixture of the same models. In fact the two are not the same, but there is an interesting relationship between their log predictive scores. In the mixture of models A_1 and A_2,

$$p(\boldsymbol{y}_t \mid \boldsymbol{Y}_{t-1}, \boldsymbol{\theta}_{A_1}, \boldsymbol{\theta}_{A_2}, w, A_{1\cdot 2}) \\ = wp(\boldsymbol{y}_t \mid \boldsymbol{Y}_{t-1}, \boldsymbol{\theta}_{A_1}) + (1-w)p(\boldsymbol{y}_t \mid \boldsymbol{Y}_{t-1}, \boldsymbol{\theta}_{A_2}). \tag{5.16}$$

Equivalently there is an i.i.d. latent binomial random variable $\tilde{w}_t$, independent of $\boldsymbol{Y}_{t-1}$, $P(\tilde{w}_t = 1) = w$, with

$$y_t \sim \begin{cases} p(\boldsymbol{y}_t \mid \boldsymbol{Y}_{t-1}, \boldsymbol{\theta}_{A_1}) & \text{if } \tilde{w}_t = 1, \\ p(\boldsymbol{y}_t \mid \boldsymbol{Y}_{t-1}, \boldsymbol{\theta}_{A_2}) & \text{if } \tilde{w}_t = 0. \end{cases}$$

If the prediction model A_j is fully Bayesian (5.1) or utilizes maximum-likelihood estimates in (5.2), then, under weak regularity conditions,

$$T^{-1}\,\mathrm{LS}(\boldsymbol{Y}_T, A_j) \\ \xrightarrow{\text{a.s.}} \lim_{T\to\infty} T^{-1} \int \log p(\boldsymbol{Y}_T \mid \boldsymbol{\theta}^*_{A_j}, A_j) p(\boldsymbol{Y}_T \mid D)\,\mathrm{d}\boldsymbol{Y}_T \\ = \mathrm{LS}^*(A_j; D) \quad (j = 1, 2),$$

where

$$\boldsymbol{\theta}^*_{A_j} = \operatorname*{argmax}_{\boldsymbol{\theta}_{A_j}} \lim_{T\to\infty} T^{-1} \int \log p(\boldsymbol{Y}_T \mid \boldsymbol{\theta}_{A_j}, A_j) \\ \cdot\, p(\boldsymbol{Y}_T \mid D)\,\mathrm{d}\boldsymbol{Y}_T \quad (j = 1, 2), \tag{5.17}$$

and these are sometimes called the pseudotrue values of $\boldsymbol{\theta}_{A_1}$ and $\boldsymbol{\theta}_{A_2}$. However, $\boldsymbol{\theta}^*_{A_1}$ and $\boldsymbol{\theta}^*_{A_2}$ are not, in general, the pseudotrue values of $\boldsymbol{\theta}_{A_1}$ and $\boldsymbol{\theta}_{A_2}$ in the mixture model $A_{1\cdot 2}$, and w^* is not the pseudotrue value of w. These values are instead

$$\{\boldsymbol{\theta}_{A_1}^{**}, \boldsymbol{\theta}_{A_2}^{**}, w^{**}\} = \operatorname*{argmax}_{\boldsymbol{\theta}_{A_1}, \boldsymbol{\theta}_{A_2}, w} \lim_{T\to\infty} T^{-1} \int \sum_{t=1}^{T} \log[w p(y_t \mid \boldsymbol{Y}_{t-1}, \boldsymbol{\theta}_{A_1}) + (1-w) p(y_t \mid \boldsymbol{Y}_{t-1}, \boldsymbol{\theta}_{A_2})] p(\boldsymbol{Y}_T \mid D)\, \mathrm{d}\boldsymbol{Y}_T. \tag{5.18}$$

Let $w^* = \operatorname{argmax}_w f(w)$. Note that

$$\begin{aligned}
&\lim_{T\to\infty} T^{-1} \int \sum_{t=1}^{T} \log[w^{**} p(y_t \mid Y_{t-1}, \boldsymbol{\theta}_{A_1}^{**}) \\
&\qquad + (1 - w^{**}) p(y_t \mid Y_{t-1}, \boldsymbol{\theta}_{A_1}^{**})] p(\boldsymbol{Y}_T \mid D)\, \mathrm{d}\boldsymbol{Y}_T \\
&\geqslant \lim_{T\to\infty} T^{-1} \int \sum_{t=1}^{T} \log[w^* p(y_t \mid Y_{t-1}, \boldsymbol{\theta}_{A_1}^{*}) \\
&\qquad + (1 - w^{*}) p(y_t \mid Y_{t-1}, \boldsymbol{\theta}_{A_1}^{*})] p(\boldsymbol{Y}_T \mid D)\, \mathrm{d}\boldsymbol{Y}_T \\
&= w^* \operatorname{LS}^*(A_j; D) + (1 - w^*) \operatorname{LS}^*(A_j; D).
\end{aligned}$$

Therefore, the best log predictive score that can be obtained from a linear pool of the models A_1 and A_2 is a lower bound on the log predictive score of a mixture model constructed from A_1 and A_2. This result clearly generalizes to pools and mixtures of n models.

To illustrate these relationships, suppose that the data-generating process D is

$$y_t \sim \begin{cases} N(1,1) & \text{if } y_{t-1} > 0, \\ N(-1,1) & \text{if } y_{t-1} < 0. \end{cases}$$

In model A_1,

$$y_t \overset{\text{i.i.d.}}{\sim} N(\mu, \sigma^2) \quad \text{with } \mu \geqslant 1,$$

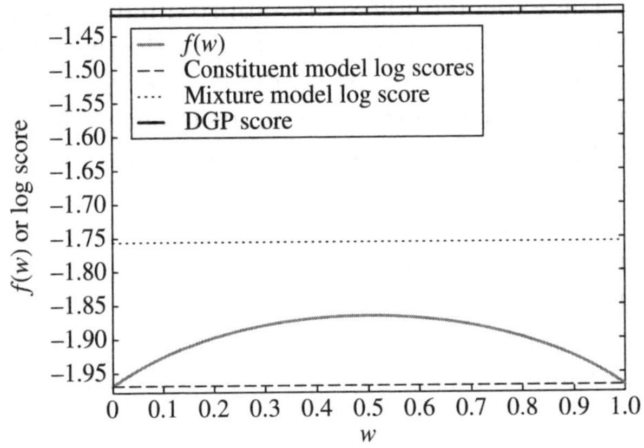

Figure 5.7. Expected log scores for individual models, a linear model pool, a mixture model, and the data-generating process.

and in model A_2,

$$y_t \overset{\text{i.i.d.}}{\sim} N(\mu, \sigma^2) \quad \text{with } \mu \leqslant -1.$$

Corresponding to (5.17) the pseudotrue value of μ is 1 in A_1 and -1 in A_2; the pseudotrue value of σ^2 is 3 in both models. The expected log score, approximated by direct simulation, is -1.974 in both models. This value is indicated by the dashed horizontal line near the bottom of figure 5.7. The function $f(w)$, also approximated by direct simulation, is indicated by the concave solid curve in the same figure. The maximum, at $w = \frac{1}{2}$, is $f(w) = -1.866$. Thus $f_T(w)$ would indicate that neither model could coincide with D, even for small T.

The mixture model (5.16) will interpret the data as independent and identically distributed, and the pseudotrue values corresponding to (5.18) will be $\mu = 1$ for one component, $\mu = -1$ for the other, and $\sigma^2 = 1$ in both. The expected log score, approximated by direct simulation, is -1.756, indicated by the dotted horizontal line in figure 5.7. In the model $A = D$, $y_t \mid (y_{t-1}, A)$ has mean -1 or 1 and variance 1. Its expected log score is $-\frac{1}{2}[\log(2\pi) - 1] = -1.419$, indicated by the solid horizontal line near the top of the figure.

The example illustrates that $\max f(w)$ can fall well short of the mixture model expected log score, and that the latter can, in turn, be much less than the data-generating process expected log score. It is never possible to show that $A = D$: only to adduce evidence that $A \neq D$.

5.7 Consequences of an Incomplete Model Space

In any decision-making setting requiring prediction there will be competing models. If one takes the model space to be complete—that is, if one conditions on one of the available models being true—then econometric theory is comparatively tidy. In both Bayesian and non-Bayesian approaches, it is typically the case that one of a fixed number of models will come to dominate as sample size increases without bound.

In social science applications, at least, there is no reason to believe that the model space is complete and in many instances there is ample evidence that it is incomplete. This chapter develops an approach to model combination designed for incomplete model spaces. It shows that linear prediction pools generally yield superior predictions as assessed by a conventional log score function. (This finding does not depend on the existence of a true model.) An important characteristic of these pools is that prediction model weights do not necessarily tend to zero or one asymptotically, as is the case for posterior probabilities. (This result invokes the existence of a true model.) The example studied here involves six models and a large sample. One of these models has a posterior probability very nearly one. Yet three of the six models in the pool have positive weights, all substantial.

Optimal log scoring of prediction pools has three practical advantages. First, it is easy to do: compared with the cost of specifying the constituent models and conducting formal inference for each, it is practically costless. Second, the behavior of the log score as a function of model weights can show clearly that the model space is incomplete. Third, linear prediction pools provide an easy way to improve predictions as assessed by the log score function. The example studied in this chapter illustrates how acknowledgment that the model space is incomplete can improve predictions, even as the search for better models goes on.

The last result is especially important. The examples in this chapter showed how models that are clearly inferior to others in the pool nevertheless substantially improve prediction if they are included as part of the pool rather than being discarded. The analytical results in section 5.4 and the examples in section 5.5 establish that the most valuable model in a pool need not be the one most strongly favored by the evidence interpreted under the assumption that one of several models is true. This lesson may well extend to decision-making contexts generally.

References

Bacharach, J. 1974. Bayesian dialogues. Unpublished manuscript, Christ Church College, Oxford University.

Bates, J. M., and C. W. J. Granger. 1969. The combination of forecasts. *Operational Research Quarterly* 20:451–68.

Berger, J. O. 2000. Bayesian analysis: a look at today and thoughts of tomorrow. *Journal of the American Statistical Association* 95: 1,269–76.

Bernardo, J. M. 1979. Expected information as expected utility. *Annals of Statistics* 7:686–90.

Bollerslev, T. 1986. Generalized autoregressive conditional heteroskedasticity. *Journal of Econometrics* 31:307–27.

——. 1988. On the correlation structure for the generalized autoregressive conditional heteroskedastic process. *Journal of Time Series Analysis* 9:121–31.

Box, G. E. P. 1980. Sampling and Bayes inference in scientific modeling and robustness. *Journal of the Royal Statistical Society* A 143:383–430.

Breiman, L. 1996. Bagging predictors. *Machine Learning* 26:123–40.

Bremmes, J. B. 2004. Probabilistic forecasts of precipitation in terms of quantiles using NWP model output. *Monthly Weather Review* 132:338–47.

Brier, G. W. 1950. Verification of forecasts expressed in terms of probability. *Monthly Weather Review* 78:1–3.

Casella, G., and R. E. Berger. 2002. *Statistical Inference*, 2nd edn. Pacific Grove, CA: Duxbury.

Chong, Y. Y., and D. F. Hendry. 1986. Econometric evaluation of linear macro-economic models. *Review of Economic Studies* 53: 671–90.

Christiano, L. J., and M. Eichenbaum. 1992. Current real-business-cycle theories and aggregate labor-market fluctuations. *American Economic Review* 82:430–50.

Christoffersen, P. F. 1998. Evaluating interval forecasts. *International Economic Review* 39:841–62.

Clemen, R. T., A. H. Murphy, and R. L. Winkler. 1995. Screening probability forecasts: contrasts between choosing and combining. *International Journal of Forecasting* 11:133–46.

Clements, M. P. 2006. Evaluating the survey of professional forecasters probability distributions of expected inflation based on derived event probability forecasts. *Empirical Economics* 31: 49–64.

Corradi, V., and N. R. Swanson. 2006a. Predictive density evaluation. In *Handbook of Economic Forecasting* (ed. G. Elliott, C. W. J. Granger, and A. Timmermann), chapter 5, pp. 197–284. Amsterdam: North-Holland.

——. 2006b. Predictive density and conditional confidence interval accuracy tests. *Journal of Econometrics* 135:187–228.

Dawid, A. P. 1984. Statistical theory: the prequential approach. *Journal of the Royal Statistical Society* A 147:278–92.

de Finetti, B., and L. J. Savage. 1963. The elicitation or personal probabilities. Unpublished manuscript.

DeGroot, M. H., and S. E. Fienberg. 1982. Assessing probability assessors: calibration and refinement. In *Statistical Decision Theory and Related Topics III* (ed. S. S. Gupta and J. O. Berger), volume 1, pp. 291–314. New York: Academic Press.

DeJong, D. N., B. F. Ingram, and C. H. Whiteman. 1996. A Bayesian approach to calibration. *Journal of Business and Economic Statistics* 14:1–10.

Diebold, F. X., T. A. Gunter, and A. S. Tay. 1998. Evaluating density forecasts with applications to financial risk management. *International Economic Review* 39:863–83.

Dueker, M. J. 1997. Markov switching in GARCH processes and mean reverting stock market volatility. *Journal of Business and Economic Statistics* 15:26–34.

Eichenbaum, M. 1991. Real business cycle theory: wisdom or whimsy? *Journal of Economic Dynamics and Control* 15:607–26.

Friedman, J., T. Hastie, and R. Tibshirani. 2000. Additive logistic regression: a statistical view of boosting. *Annals of Statistics* 28:337–74.

Gelman, A., X. L. Meng, and H. Stern. 1996. Posterior predictive assessment of model fitness via realized discrepancies. *Statistica Sinica* 6:733–807.

Genest, C., S. Weerahandi, and J. V. Zidek. 1984. Aggregating opinions through logarithmic pooling. *Theory and Decision* 17: 61–70.

Geweke, J. 1986. Discussion of "Modeling conditional variance" (T. Bollerslev and R. Engle). *Econometric Reviews* 5(1):57–61.

——. 2001. A note on some limitations of CRRA utility. *Economics Letters* 71:341–46.

——. 2005. *Contemporary Bayesian Econometrics and Statistics.* Hoboken, NJ: John Wiley.

——. 2007. Bayesian model momparison and validation. *American Economic Review Papers and Proceedings* 97:60–64.

Geweke, J., and G. Amisano. Forthcoming. Hierarchical Markov normal mixture models with applications to financial asset returns. *Journal of Applied Econometrics*, in press.

Geweke, J., and S. Porter-Hudak. 1984. The estimation and application of long memory time series models. *Journal of Time Series Analysis* 4:221–38.

Gneiting, T., and A. E. Raftery. 2007. Strictly proper scoring rules, prediction and estimation. *Journal of the American Statistical Association* 102:359–78.

Gneiting, T., F. Balabdaoul, and A. E. Raftery. 2007. Probability forecasts, calibration and sharpness. *Journal of the Royal Statistical Society* B 69:243–68.

Good, I. J. 1952. Rational decisions. *Journal of the Royal Statistical Society* B 14:107–14.

——. 1956. The surprise index for the multivariate normal distribution. *Annals of Mathematical Statistics* 27:1,130–35.

Gourieroux, C., and A. Monfort. 1989. *Statistics and Econometric Models*, volume 2. Cambridge: Cambridge University Press.

Granger, C. W. J., H. White, and M. Kamstra. 1989. Interval forecasting: an analysis based upon ARCH-quantile estimators. *Journal of Econometrics* 40:87–96.

Greenberg, E. 2007. *Introduction to Bayesian Econometrics.* Cambridge: Cambridge University Press.

Gregory, A. W., and G. W. Smith. 1991. Calibration as testing: inference in simulated macroeconomic models. *Journal of Business and Economic Statistics* 9:297–304.

Hall, S. G., and J. Mitchell. 2007. Combining density forecasts. *International Journal of Forecasting* 23:1–13.

He, C. L., and T. Terasvirta. 1999. Properties of a family of GARCH processes. *Journal of Econometrics* 92:173–92.

Hendry, D. F. 1995. *Dynamic Econometrics.* Oxford: Oxford University Press.

Hurwicz, L. 1962. On the structural form of interdependent systems. In *Logic, Methodology and the Philosophy of Science* (ed. E. Nagel), pp. 232–39. Stanford, CA: Stanford University Press.

Jacobs, R. A. 1995. Methods for combining experts' probability assessments. *Neural Computation* 7:867–88.

Jacquier, E., N. G. Polson, and P. E. Rossi. 1994. Bayesian analysis of stochastic volatility models. *Journal of Business and Economic Statistics* 12:371–89.

King, R. G., C. I. Plosser, and S. T. Rebelo. 1988. Production, growth and business cycles. II. New directions. *Journal of Monetary Economics* 21:309–41.

——. 1990. Production, growth and business cycles: technical appendix. Mimeo, University of Rochester.

Kloek, T., and H. K. van Dijk. 1978. Bayesian estimates of equation system parameters: an application of integration by Monte Carlo. *Econometrica* 46:1–20.

Kocherlakota, N. 1996. The equity premium: it's still a puzzle. *Journal of Economic Literature* 34:42–71.

Koop, G. 2003. *Bayesian Econometrics.* Chichester, UK: John Wiley.

Kydland, F. E., and E. C. Prescott. 1996. The computational experiment: an econometric tool. *Journal of Economic Perspectives* 10(1):69–86.

Labadie, P. 1989. Stochastic inflation and the equity premium. *Journal of Monetary Economics* 24:277–98.

Lancaster, T. 2004. *An Introduction to Modern Bayesian Econometrics.* Malden, MA: Blackwell.

Leamer, E. E. 1978. *Specification Searches: Ad Hoc Inference with Nonexperimental Data.* New York: John Wiley.

Little, R. J. 2006. Calibrated Bayes: a Bayes/frequentist roadmap. *The American Statistician* 60:213–23.

McConway, K. J. 1981. Marginalization and linear opinion pools. *Journal of the American Statistical Association* 76:410–14.

Mehra, R., and E. C. Prescott. 1985. The equity premium: a puzzle. *Journal of Monetary Economics* 15:145–61.

Nelson, D. 1991. Conditional heteroskedasticity in asset returns: a new approach. *Econometrica* 59:347–70.

Poirier, D. J. 1988. Frequentist and subjectivist perspectives on the problems of model building in economics. *Journal of Economic Perspectives* 2(1):121–44.

——. 1995. *Intermediate Statistics and Econometrics: A Comparative Approach.* Cambridge, MA: MIT Press.

Quandt, R. E. 1974. A comparison of methods for testing nonnested hypotheses. *Review of Economics and Statistics* 56:92–99.

Rietz, T. A. 1988. The equity premium: a solution. *Journal of Monetary Economics* 22:17–33.

Roberts, H. V. 1965. Probabilistic prediction. *Journal of the American Statistical Association* 60:50–62.

Rossi, P. E., G. Allenby, and R. McCulloch. 2005. *Bayesian Statistics and Marketing.* Hoboken, NJ: John Wiley.

Shuford, E. H., A. Albert, and H. E. Massengill. 1966. Admissible probability measurement procedures. *Psychometrika* 31:125–45.

Smith, A. A. 1993. Estimating nonlinear time series models using simulated vector autoregressions. *Journal of Applied Econometrics* 8:S63–S84.

Stone, M. 1961. The opinion pool. *Annals of Mathematical Statistics* 32:1,339–42.

Timmermann, A. 2006. Forecast combination. In *Handbook of Economic Forecasting* (ed. G. Elliott, C. W. J. Granger, and A. Timmermann), chapter 4, pp. 135–96. Amsterdam: North-Holland.

Tsionas, E. G. 2005. Likelihood evidence on the asset returns puzzle. *Review of Economic Studies* 72:917–46.

Wallis, K. F. 2005. Combining density and interval forecasts: a modest proposal. *Oxford Bulletin of Economics and Statistics* 67:983–94.

Watson, M. W. 1993. Measures of fit for calibrated models. *Journal of Political Economy* 101:1,011–41.

Winkler, R. L. 1969. Scoring rules and the evaluation of probability assessors. *Journal of the American Statistical Association* 64:1,073–78.

Winkler, R. L., and A. M. Murphy. 1968. "Good" probability assessors. *Journal of Applied Meteorology* 7:751–58.

Zellner, A. 1971. *An Introduction to Bayesian Inference in Econometrics and Statistics.* New York: John Wiley.